D1277073

WORD AND REDEMPTION

WORD
AND REDEMPTION

Essays in Theology 2

HANS URS VON BALTHASAR

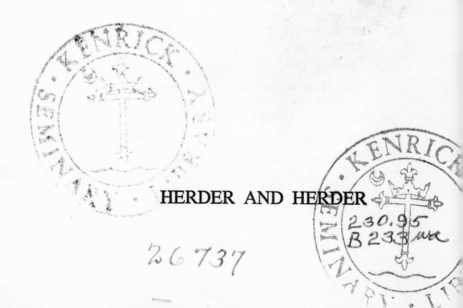

HERDER AND HERDER

1965
HERDER AND HERDER NEW YORK
232 Madison Avenue, New York 10016

Translated by A. V. Littledale in cooperation with
Alexander Dru. Original edition: *Verbum Caro.*
Skizzen zur Theologie I, second part (Johannes Verlag Einsiedeln).

Nihil obstat: Patrick A. Barry
             Censor Librorum

Imprimatur: ✠ Robert F. Joyce, Bishop of Burlington
             December 9, 1964

Library of Congress Catalog Card Number: 65-14591

CONTENTS

THE PLACE OF THEOLOGY

1

The Word that is God became man, without ceasing to be God. The Word that is infinite became finite, without ceasing to be infinite. The Word that is God took a body of flesh, in order to be man. And because he is Word, and, as Word, took flesh, he took on, at the same time, a body consisting of syllables, scripture, ideas, images, verbal utterance and preaching, since otherwise men would not have understood either that the Word really was made *flesh,* or that the divine Person who was made flesh was really the *Word.* All scriptural problems must be approached through christology: the letter is related to the Spirit as the flesh of Christ (we know what that means: his human nature) to his divine nature and Person.

In the factual order this means that the flesh and its manifestation are of no avail, if we do not reach through the flesh to the Spirit (see Paul), if, in the flesh, we do not hear, see, feel after the Spirit (see John). The letter is important and worthy of attention insofar as it can be a bridge to the Spirit, and the finiteness of human concepts, images and words, insofar as they can afford us access to the infinity of the divine Logos. And in the order of knowledge this means that an initial attitude to revelation in flesh and letter is right only if we are always prepared to be led through the finiteness of flesh and the letter to the infinity of the divine truth, which is one with the divine Person of the Son (inseparable from, and essentially one with the Father and the Spirit). The true preparation is faith. Faith is the surrender of the finite person in his entirety to the infinite Person. Where value is concerned, particularly where truth and knowledge are concerned, however, that same surrender is love, which in the temporal structure of existence (and the various modes of its intersection with the eternity indwelling there) reveals itself as hope.

There are two contrasting forms of existence. There is the existence of an infinite Person, who is the Word, within the flesh and the earthly and finite embodiment of his divine and infinite fullness. For the Word as flesh is a Word that is lived to the very limit, and, where the flesh takes the form of the letter, it is filled to the very limit with Spirit—filled not only with divine and infinite content, but with a divine and human content, lived, that is to say, in the bodily existence of Christ. The other existence is that of the believer, insofar as faith (a grace given by the infinite Person) is, for men, the only thing adequate to the incarnate God. Surrender to the Infinite, surrender that knows no limits in principle, is the initial attitude possible to man which prepares the way for the finite factors of revelation, flesh and the letter, to be understood as what they really are, namely as the utterance and expression of the Infinite.

This surrender implies, in the first place, an absolute will and readiness to encounter God in what is human, and the infinite content in the finite concept. It is, therefore, an

8

attitude of adoration; from the very outset, one approaches the word of God, the scripture, on one's knees, prostrate, in the conviction that the written word has within it the spirit and power to bring about, in faith, contact with the infinity of the Word. It has this power all the more because the word of scripture is not prior to the cross—flesh, that is to say, in the Old Testament sense, allowing its inner divine content to appear only exceptionally, as on Tabor—but a word subsequent to the cross—flesh that has risen, the letter already steeped in the infinity and glory of God. Nor is it a word that the resurrection has passed over, leaving no trace on it, so that the inner form and letter of the New Testament could be placed alongside that of the Old, as though the two were on a level. On the contrary, its very essence is to witness to the resurrection; even more, it is a word of the risen Christ (who, in those forty days, interpreted to the Church both himself and the Old Testament), who poured his spiritualized humanity, his finitude now rendered infinite, into the mold of an utterance accessible to us, a sequence of finite concepts. This word we can only encounter in an attitude of adoration which not only acknowledges its absolute rightness over and above all human views, contrary or not, but on principle causes all finite perceptions and interpretations to be surmounted and filled out by an infinite range of meanings.

In the second place, the surrender in question means the will to make this infinite meaning (to which no knowledge in time can attain) the ground of one's own existence ("Be it done to me according to thy word"), that is to say, not only to live in the presence of the Word, but to live by its power and in view of it. The Word is a Word lived to the

9

utmost limit, incarnated, put to death, resurrected and, now glorified, at once infinite and finite, guiding, from above and within, the entire existence of the man surrendered to it in faith; so much so that, in his life, he perceives what the life of Christ is, both in him and in itself, and his own life becomes a witness and echo of the Word in time. In the holiness of the communion of saints the world should come to learn what the holiness (that is, the divineness) of the incarnate Word on earth was. Without this holiness of the Word we live by, the holiness of the Word we worship would lack full incarnational truth. The Word in the world has the power to turn speculative truth into actual living, the exercise of authority into holiness of life, theology into Christian practice, reflection into irrefutable witness of life to the point of martyrdom. This is what its credentials consist in, but they derive ultimately from men's utter surrender to it and adoration in faith, hope and love to the indwelling Word.

Whatever external graces and "signs" the Church has been endowed with by her founder are not ends in themselves, but means to the above-mentioned end and incentives to its attainment. The infused holiness of the Church as "institution" is simply the source and starting point of the interior and practical holiness of the Christian, which is what her founder intended thereby. Her given unity, made visible in the hierarchy, is simply the basis for that living, perfect unity of love which inwardly sustains and builds up the body of Christ. The totality (catholicity) of the truth and love implanted in her by her founder must be continuously unfolded in fullness of life by the workings of the Holy Spirit; apostolicity, the exterior uninterrupted suc-

10

cession in time, is simply the guarantee and starting point for all generations of Christians, of an ever-fresh and immediate relation to the apostles and, through them, to Christ, an incentive to seek this ever anew and to renew the apostolic witness by their own holiness of life. To call these "means" is not to say that, once the end is reached, they can be discarded. They are part of the structure of the Church in the world and, so long as she retains her present form, so long must they endure. But when this structure passes away, the means also pass away; already they have within themselves an element directing them to what is quite other, and alone an end in itself: adoration and holiness, in other words, love of God and one's neighbor.

This applies to the whole official side of the Church. Thus it applies equally to theology, insofar as it is something other than direct adoration of the divine Word in the finite word, other than the act of direct obedience to the Word in the Christian life. To that extent therefore, and lying between these two interdependent poles of the Christian's intercourse with the Word of God, there is intercalated something which might be called theorizing about the Word of God—a form of contemplation which is neither an act of worship nor conjoined with action wherein the truth is embodied. Like all the modes in which the Church sets forth her teaching, theology can only be oriented toward these two poles, and so toward the purity and fullness of the Church's teaching, with which it partially coincides. For, while being a special form of the Church's teaching (the theologian, too, has an official role), theology is, at the same time, a function, a corrective, a preliminary to the official teaching. Together with this latter and the sacraments, theology is a means, an active agency for pouring the infinite riches of divine truth into the finite vessels in which revelation is given to us, so that the believer may be made capable of encountering this infinity in adoration and active obedience. Revealed truth, since it is both divine truth and the truth we live by, is so constituted that the amount of truth in theology (as it prepares the way to worship and a life of obedience) must be measured in terms of worship and practical obedience. For Christ is no theory, not even insofar as he is the truth (not the truth as human knowledge is true). The flame of worship and obedience must burn through the dispassionateness of speculation, as it always does through the entire Word of God: the Word that was Christ, and that gave itself to be consumed in this same fire; the word that once again is Christ and is called "scripture," the letter aglow with the Spirit and fire, scorching those who approach it without first taking off their shoes.

Now, in the very fact of God's existence in the flesh, there must be a level on which the word of God (since it is a truly human word) meets with other human words. This is the level of disputation, of argument. This level is laid open to being controverted, to arguments for and against, to the cavils and quibbles of the Scribes, to the groping incomprehension of the disciples, to the doubtings of the fearful, who "see men as trees" (Mk 8:24). God's word here always speaks with the same infinite superiority that characterized it in the Old Testament, but always in the same human situation. It lets itself enter into human contact and man's concerns. It lays itself open to contradiction, to argumentation, to syllogistic and theological deduction. Coming out into the open, it denudes itself. In this consists the abasement of

12

the Word, from the very beginning, that so stirred Hamann that he made it the center of his theology: the condescension not only of the Lord to the status of servant, but of the sovereign Spirit to the servitude of the letter, and this in the very act of creation, culminating in his embodiment in the Church. Yet it must always be borne in mind that this concession to human understanding is only made for the purpose of leading it away from its own natural level to that of faith and to a corresponding decision. Futhermore (and this is very clear in John), all theological dispute with the Word is a stage on the way either to the act of faith or of disbelief. The argument with the Samaritan woman, the adulteress, the man born blind, is itself of redemptive import, leading to an act of total adoration in the person involved; that with the Jews is itself a severance of relations, a judgment on the obduracy of the disputants; and, for this reason, the passion of the Word in John is, at this point, already in course of enactment. These are the hours of darkness, when the light shines in the night of man's refusal to understand. They are the first stage in the killing of the divine Word, the beginnings of a philology that has no intention of issuing in adoration and obedience, but is sufficient to itself. "Your testimony is not true." They are a theology which, while it takes up stones, goes on speaking. And we see how the apparent neutrality of disputation looks from the standpoint of God's eternal decree. No prolonged dwelling in the stage of theory is permitted the Church's theology, any more than to the Jews in their contact with the Word of God. Not for a single moment can theology forget its roots, from which all its nourishment is drawn: adoration, in which we see, in faith, the heavens opened; and obedience in living, which frees us to understand the truth.

2

From what we have said above, many conclusions follow regarding the structure of theology. In the first place, a general truth: that in theology all that has to do with the finite aspect of the Word (with concepts, images, the letter) must be considered solely a means to reaching the infinity incarnated therein. There is urgent need of a thorough investigation into the formal logic of the mode of speech and thought of the Word of God. This would of necessity bring out how the formal laws of human speech and thought are in no way superseded, but rather carried up to a higher plane, since all the laws applying to what is finite become functions of a truth infinite in every "part" or manifestation, and not susceptible of being parceled into finite dictums and laws. Such an investigation would bear many points of resemblance to that of Bultmann, and yet would be very different. It would not approach the Word of God through any philosophic, existential presuppositions, but would be developed from the basic fact of the incarnation (accepted in faith). It cannot be said that, through the incarnation, or even through the resurrection, human "flesh" (human nature with all its laws of finite being and thought) has been "relativized." That would be, once again, a category of this world, finite and wholly inadequate for this absolutely unique, unparallelled event. This is why modernism, though often near the mark, was basically off-target.

Neither history nor evolution nor philosophy has the

14

Word for its province, but faith alone, which requires that theology be presented in such a way as to foster a more profound spirit of adoration, a more exact obedience in practice. The theologian, therefore, is required to apply the laws of human thinking in such a way as to bring out clearly the law of faith. The laws of thought are primarily concerned with drawing limits, defining, even if this is done so as subsequently to interrelate more precisely the fields thus delimited. So long as the various contents of truth are themselves finite, there is nothing to object to in this process of defining and contrasting. The case is otherwise when the laws of faith come into action, for then the truth comprised within the drawn limits is the same (not only generically, but substantially and personally) as the truth outside them. The drawing of the boundary does not involve falsehood (for it is all part of the movement of the Word's incarnation), provided that one is always aware of the presence, within the boundary, of the unbounded, the presence in the concept of what is beyond concept, in the definition of the presence of the divine object of faith. And this applies even more to the subsequent operations in which this first delimited sphere (of infinite content) is brought into relation with others (also of infinite content).

In other words, every concept in theology must be catholic, universal, which means it must present the whole truth, either by drawing it into itself or by opening itself out thereto, discarding its own boundaries, dying in order to rise again into the truth which is of heaven. This is the work of faith, not of an Hegelian dialect of knowledge; it is the work of a knowledge that is itself a faith which seeks, and then finds according to the measure of adoration, obedience and

15

grace. A catholic concept is by no means the same as a Platonist or Aristotelian one, for the simple reason that God's Word in human form (flesh or scripture) is not just any kind of word. The "inclusiveness" or "openness" that is the essence of catholic logic does not authorize us to allow everything to drift away into a kind of vague infinity, as furthering devotion. On the contrary, it is the most stringent requirement in thinking there could be. It demands that our thinking should be continuously and deliberately subject to the Word of God not only in its content, but also in its form, in the very act of thought—which must, perforce, bear the mark of catholic logic. Theology is the expression of the verdict passed by the divine word over the human. This is, in fact, the form taken, from the beginning, by the entire word of scripture; and it is impossible for theology to evade this form.

From this general characteristic follows the detail of theology, its material.

1. This material, in its whole range, its basic structure, its essential features, must be governed according to revelation, and this in the way in which it actually was given in history—or, more precisely, as it happened historically within the human race and is described in scripture. This means, in the first place, that theology has to understand and interpret the divine content in this history and not leave it to one side while drawing from it an unhistorical, supratemporal (and thus not truly eternal) "moral of history." The incarnation is no mere "figure" of a truth, but truth itself. It means, further, that theology has to consider this history (for even the didactic parts of the Old and New Testaments are a function of the history) in its essential

course, and not simply in certain episodes or concepts chosen at will. Scripture is not a quarry out of which theology can hew individual sentences to suit its purpose. It is the witness of a total event, a unity in itself; and it is as a totality that it is the object of theology.

The proportions of the structure of theology must be governed by those of revelation, that is to say, not of scripture as a book, but of the event described in scripture. The Holy Spirit is always sovereign in this sphere; he breathes where he will, leads into all truth in the way he chooses, and throws his light on the meaning of the Word in the sources of revelation according to his will. Therefore we must always read scripture in the light of the Spirit (the Spirit of the Church and of Catholicism). This does not imply that the theologian is entitled to settle down comfortably in some corner, to specialize there, without further concern with the totality of revelation. There is, of course, bound to be specialization, owing to the limitations of science. But the difference between theology and other sciences is that in the former the object is not a finite one, corresponding to the limitations of our powers. And there is another, even more important difference: whereas in other sciences progress consists in increasing differentiation and refinement of the subject matter, here the work leads further and further in the direction of the infinity that pertains to the object, which has presented itself to us in a finite form adapted to our understanding. A man can write on theology without being obliged to deal with the whole of it; but he must always preserve the totality, the catholicity of truth in every detail of his thought.

However important mariology may be in these times, one

17

cannot escape the impression that it affords a welcome excuse for theologians to avoid subjects which, if the proportions of revelation are to be preserved, demand greater
attention, but also more courage and expository skill. The
doctrines of the Trinity, of the incarnation, of the redemption,
of the resurrection, of predestination and eschatology bristle
with problems that all too often we prefer to bypass. Such
an attitude is inexcusable. The thought of previous generations (even if it has resulted in conciliar definitions) is
never a pillow for future thought to rest on. Definitions are
not so much an end as a beginning. Nothing that is the fruit
of hard struggle is ever lost to the Church, but this does not
mean that the theologian is spared further work. Whatever is
merely put in storage, handed down without any fresh
efforts being made on one's own part (and *ab ovo*, the
very source of revelation) putrifies, like the manna did.
And the longer the living tradition has been broken through
purely mechanical repetition, the more difficult it may become to renew it.

2. The whole span of revelation, which provides the
basic dimension of theology, broadens as theology becomes
the regulative principle not of a timeless, but of a contemporary preaching and teaching of the word. This does not, of
course, mean that theology must adopt a servile and
timerous attitude toward current fashions of thought, so as
to "keep abreast of the times" (for example, by becoming
existentialist or by demythologizing), or that it should
provide an apologetic palatable to modern man, but that, in
obedience to its own inmost law, it should attend to the
light which the Holy Ghost sheds here and now on revealed
truth. The Spirit who breathes where he will is not the mild,

diffused, timeless beacon of the Enlightenment always present in the same fashion. Rather he is the Spirit of missions and special functions within the mystical body, the Spirit who, in fulfilling the Old Testament, continues its historical course, in which ever new, unforseeable tasks sent by God erupt. It would indeed be all too simple (and a complete justification of Buber's penetrating objections) if the Christian could ignore the tremendous and inescapable unrest created in us by a revelation at once contemporaneous and leading into the future, and could live on in the past, that forever is sinking further into the past. Yet who, if not the theologian, is the watchman on the tower ready to proclaim the hour not of world history, but of Christian history, reading for us today the signs in the meridian light of eternal revelation?

There are, of course, many signs by which to read and interpret and to discern the spirits. There are, first of all, the different kinds of sanctity and of missions conferred on a given epoch, which may in turn call attention to the modes of sanctity of earlier times and, in the light of the present and its needs, make them more comprehensible. Those who truly adore and are truly obedient are those in whom the present truth of the Word is most clearly embodied. Their life is doctrine put into practice; and if they have a special mission in life, it throws an especially actual and God-intended light on doctrine. It is a light of the Spirit, illuminating the light of the Son. There is no question of persons involved, still less any question of psychology or biography, but rather one of the intrinsic content of mission, insofar as it is the voice, the word and the light of God for the times. /

19

The same light will not be withheld from the theologian himself, provided that, in his work, he draws on the spirit of adoration and obedience. It is the self-same light that unfailingly guides the teaching authority (and thereby points the way for the individual theologian), on condition that, also for the official leaders of the Church and community, it is a light sought for in prayer and suffering, and not simply borrowed, something taken out of storage. Here we come up against profound and terrible mysteries concerning the Church: the "angels of the churches" are under the most severe judgment of the Lord of the Church, for this Lord does not tolerate any complacent dependence on office alone, any decline in initial fervor and love, but demands the utmost zeal of watchman and shepherd. The theologian who lets himself be guided by authority must have an especially strong sense of his own responsibility toward the teaching authority, for, if he is exercised thoroughly in obedience to the Spirit, his own suggestions, emendations, his general view or new insight may have an important part to play in the formulation of doctrine and its promulgation.

3. The third and most difficult question can now be approached, that of the relation between revelation today (1 and 2) and tradition yesterday, a relation resulting in tradition today. Its difficulty stems from the fact that, since tradition must always remain a living principle, the theology of all past ages has to be incorporated as a living thing, it being remembered that the guidance of the Spirit yesterday is not identical with that of today; in fact, insofar as it was guidance for a particular situation in the past, it cannot be applicable to the present.

20

This does not mean we must look with suspicion at the formulations, the systems and worldviews of the theology of the past. Suspicion is an unprofitable attitude and the reverse of inclusive. What it does mean, what it requires, is that the theology of today must have such a certainty and fullness—derived from the eternal fullness of revelation, of the Spirit given at this time, and of the fullness of the tradition received—as to embrace the riches of past theology as a living thing, and to endow it with fresh vitality. But if the theologian of today is to preserve a living contact with the tradition of yesterday, he has the grave responsibility of conjoining his reverence for the abiding words of the fathers, the scholastics, the spiritual writers with an un-dimmed view of the temporal element from which none are exempt.

Nothing brings so much harm in its train as the failure to appreciate an historical context. It is bound adversely to affect the theology of the present. It is an ostrich-like pro-ceeding—with this difference, that the ostrich, in hiding its head in the sand, counts on not being seen at all, whereas the theologian, hiding in the sands of timelessness, hopes, despite his disregard of history, to be taken account of by history. What is required is neither an enthusiastic revival of something or other (for example, the "fathers"), nor pure historical research, but rather that kind of Christian human-ism that goes to the sources to find what is living and truly original (and not to a school of thought long since dried up), in a spirit of joy and freedom able to weigh the true value of things. This is the spirit from which we may hope for a tradition that is truly contemporary.

Like all good things in the world, the capacity to hand

21

down requires a full measure of freedom, responsibility and Christian audacity. We can see this very clearly in the way in which St. Paul handed down what was delivered to him. Anyone without that capacity who wants to form a link in the chain of tradition, and hands down the goods of theology more or less like a workman passing bricks from hand to hand so that they are least likely to be damaged, is profoundly misled—simply because thoughts are not bricks; and, besides, since the first Easter morning, the fight between Spirit and stone, the stone which held the body captive, has not slackened.

These three lines of reflection serve, simply, to mark out a space, and to incite theology to build on it. Having seen it, one finds it difficult to understand why so few theologians have attempted the task; and even those few have applied themselves to only a section of the edifice, and left the main part alone. It is useless to look to theological commissions; their business is to point out what is defective. We need individuals who devote their lives to the glory of theology, that fierce fire burning in the dark night of adoration and obedience, whose abysses it illuminates.

CHARACTERISTICS OF CHRISTIANITY

If Christ were no more than the supreme example of natural man, and Christianity only the noblest form of natural religion, it would now no longer be worthwhile being a Christian. Our assessment of what belongs to history is subject to fluctuation, and some past or future person might dispute Christ's preeminence. Since in Christ God became man, Christianity is bound, in the eyes of unbelievers, to seem merely human. But for the believer this view is not simply a partial misunderstanding; it is a complete misapprehension, a scandal, however solemnly and religiously it be expressed, as in the act of the high priest rending his garments, when he heard the answer of Christ. For faith, all human religions and philosophical systems seem to approximate to one another, and Christianity seems to become more and more isolated. However variegated the shopwindow display of philosophies of life may seem, from a distance they come to look very much alike, all equally of human provenance and human proportions.

Their scale, however, is limited, and likewise their application. What man can achieve unaided, what he can discover and sketch out in the way of a philosophy of life can be surveyed and grasped in its general lines, even if not in all its details, and classified. However bold his mental flights, whether in a dirigible or a rocket, he invariably takes himself along on the journey. In other words, human thought, philosophical or religious, starts out from man, ascends with him, operates on his scale. This does not thereby make it "immanent in the world," confined to man and his world. It is, in fact, in his intention, "world-transcending" in the sense of Pascal: *L'homme passe infiniment l'homme.* Yet however much man transcends himself, the act of transcending is, as the word betrays, an act posited, ventured, in reference to man. Even when he negates himself in order to affirm the other, he can only understand the affirmation in relation to what he negates.

It would be a want of gratitude to the Creator to represent this power of transcending as nugatory, this mode of contact with what is beyond the world as a mere *fabrica idolorum,* and necessarily blasphemous. But it would be equally lacking in gratitude to the redeemer and giver of grace not to see in grace something wholly new and other, crowning and perfecting man's attempts, precisely because it first shatters and overturns them. The natural man and his reason go out beyond themselves, they are "transcending"; God's grace, which we take hold of in faith, is something indwelling: and in that sense "immanent." It is not our movement toward God, but God's movement to us. It is heaven projected into our world. It is a participation in the divine nature, essentially as sanctifying grace, consciously as faith, hope and charity. The natural man is man seeking God, grace is God who has found man. The former is the man who applies himself to a kind of spectral analysis of his own being so as to deduce therefrom the composition

24

of the star from which he has proceeded as if by radiation, and with which he must have some sort of kinship. The latter is the descent of the divine light among men not only to illuminate, purify and warm them, but, through grace, to make them also shine with a light not of this world. It should never be forgotten that these two movements are in opposite directions. It is true that the first is for the sake of the second, and so is, in some way, a condition of it; also that the first cannot be understood, in the Creator's design, apart from the second, which is its justification and the solution to its riddles. But all this belongs to another part of the inquiry, and we shall return to it at the end.

Before making a synthesis, it is necessary to distinguish what is to be united. Otherwise, if we carry over, just as they are, the categories and conclusions of philosophy into the sphere of faith and theology, we do a disservice to both, divinizing what is secular, and secularizing what is divine. The work of synthesis, moreover, is not to be carried out on the abstract plane, by speculating on the relation between the natural and the supernatural; it is ultimately a matter of christology. For in Christ, God and man, God has opened himself to the world, and in this movement of descent has determined the course of every mode of ascent of man to him. Christ is the one and only criterion, given in the concrete, by which we measure the relations between God and man, grace and nature, faith and reason; and Christ is, though he has a human nature, a divine Person. This is the determining factor in the relationships. His humanity is the expression and instrument of the divinity, and by no means is the divinity the expression and instrument of the humanity. In every respect, the humanity is fulfilled

25

in that it sees itself, with all its upward stirrings, brought into the service of God's revelation, into the downward movement of his grace and love./

The peculiarity of the standpoint of faith in contrast with that of reason will be brought out by three examples, all converging from different directions into the one center.

1

Created being is characterized by an inner tension, a non-identity, which has been described by Thomism in recent years as a "real distinction" between essence and existence. This tension of finite being, as created, is not its own existence, but receives it, or, in other words, never realizes its essence in its totality, but is always in process of becoming. This is what distinguishes the creature from the divine being, always perfectly fulfilled, absolutely identical with itself—a contrast greater than any similarity between them, *in tanta similitudine major dissimilitudo.* It is a distinction not merely to our way of thinking, but inherent in the very being of things—*distinctio realis,* or, at least, *cum fundamento in realitate,* which, taken seriously, leads to the first—and sets its stamp on the whole *life* of the finite being, and lies at the root of its structure as indicated by Aristotle: the tension between act and potency in its living, moving dynamism of charged potentiality and self-realizing actuality, and always a tension which is a striving toward an end: *entelecheia.* If this life is *spirit,* its basic constitution may be conceived in the following categories: on the theoretical plane, it moves between the poles: potentiality— actuality, ideal—reality; on the practical plane between the

26

poles: value—being, obligation—performance. Now if the concept of entelechy also implies that "ideality" and obligation are not extraneous to being, but deeply embedded in reality and being, then the movement and tension spring from some lack, some shortcoming in this reality, making it reach out beyond itself. For it to be and remain in being, it must become; become what it is, and yet, since it is becoming, is not yet; to maintain itself it must strive, and, in striving, fulfill its own law. This law, insofar as unfulfilled, is abstract; if it is to become living in the concrete, it must be realized anew in each individual. The life of the created spirit is only vigorous when it is constantly in process of self-realization; it starts to languish the moment it becomes satisfied with what it has already attained. Even what it has in fact inherited it must win for itself, in order to possess it. Only as an incomplete indigent life is it a parable of eternal life, as intended by the Creator. Thus, in its very striving, in that very dissimilar act, is it similar to the nonstriving, eternally fulfilled life of God.

God, however, in giving us his grace and infusing, along with it, faith, hope and charity gives us a participation in his eternal life, something beyond all the life of striving which is that of the creature. Eternal life, the unattainable end of all human striving, is opened up to us in grace and made present. "He that believes has eternal life." He has it in faith, not in vision, but he has it not only eschatologically, as promised, but also as a present reality. Through grace, he is a son of God not only in the future, but here and now; he is not only called to be, but is a brother of Christ. It is a grace of sonship and brotherhood that he has received, making him a new creature, born again, transplanted, causing him to die to himself for Christ to live in him. It places deep in his heart the witness of the Holy Spirit, testifying this sonship to his own spirit, and so he no longer lives of and for himself, but by the power of Christ and of God, by God's love which is poured out into his heart by the Holy Spirit. He lives, henceforth, by Christ's love, given him so that he may love his brethren by the power of this love, give his life for them, as Christ the redeemer did. Grace is indeed not separative, but unitive. It would be an incorrect emphasis to say that "only" by grace are we what Christ is by nature, namely sons of God, as though grace created a disparity. What we ought to say is that grace is so great that we, out of pure grace, in our own way, may claim to be what Christ, the giver of grace, is by nature in his singular way.

The divine nature being necessarily transcendent, the creature's participation in it can only be explained by taking as our starting point the hypostatic union in Christ. Christ is unique in that he is not one creature among all the others, on a par with them; this is witnessed to by the overshadowing of the Holy Spirit and signified by the virginity of his mother. His creaturely status is an expression and function of his eternal and uncreated sonship. This is the real ground and justification of the Council of Ephesus' anti-Nestorian definition of μία φύσις even when taken in conjunction with the Chalcedonian δύο φύσεις. /In virtue of the hypostatic union the eternal Son of man (under the law of the real distinction) can represent the Trinity in the world. The extent to which he does so (Jn 1:18) has not yet been sufficiently explored in theology. This, however, is not our present concern, which is rather to bring out that the whole

28

of Christian ethics must be christologically based and, therefore, does not primarily consist in the Greek idea of man imitating God (μίμησις θεοῦ), but in the gospel idea of the following of Christ (ἀκολουθέω, for which scripture, significantly enough, has no adequate corresponding substantive).

Following Christ, after first leaving all things, means in the New Testament a movement toward the Messiah, at once unconditional and regardless of consequences, an inchoate act of presence where he is, developing, when and as he wills, into an imitation of him. The saying about bearing one's cross is an extreme case of this; but even here the word used to describing it is "following" and not "imitation." Whenever following implies imitation, it is always in respect of the way divine love abased itself. The word occurs once in the synoptics in connection with the strife for the first places, once in John in connection with the washing of the feet; in addition, there is the use of the word "example" in the final discourses, referring to the giving up of life. Yet however urgently the commandment of love is expressed, how undemanding, in fact, what is commanded! It is something far less than heroic, something plain and obvious, though the persons addressed have the status of "followers," which means of participators in the mystery of the hypostatic union. For what has to be done is already performed, as to its inner substance, in the Head.

What the Head does is certainly the unimaginably greatest thing that a man has ever done. Yet it is not superhuman, but divine-human, and so all-human—not however, in the sense that all men do it or can do it, but that it represents, once and for all, what God is as distinct from man, and what he created man in order to express. "Ὑπὲρ οὐσία σύσιώθη.

29

Ἐν τοῖς φυσικοῖς ἡμῶν ὑπερφυὴς ἦν (Denis). Of him we have to predicate each of these pairs of opposites: effort to obey and unquestioning obedience, real temptation and the impossibility of yielding, profound dereliction and inseparability from the Father. Here is the abyss of tragedy beyond all tragedy.

We are not required to repeat, on our part, what Christ, God and man, has done. It is enough for us to know in following him that we participate in his riches through their superabundance.

The natural virtues are acquired by effort on the natural plane. The supernatural virtues are infused through grace, which is a participation in the nature of God. They are the form in which our finite spirit becomes capable of living the divine life, which is infinite. What it is endowed with, infused with, is not just a "faculty," but a fullness of life, from which it only has to draw in order to water the entire garden of its finitude and temporalness, and so make eternal growths come forth. Thus the soul in grace does not live in a state of indigence advancing toward fullness, but in a state of fullness radiating out into the poverty and darkness of this world. The Lord is the light of the world, and it is given the soul to be its light together with him. All that was said about the essential constitution of the finite has become for the moment of no importance; for the just man lives by faith, that is, by the gift of eternal life. His acts are performed not as part of his striving toward perfection, but as proceeding from perfection; and not in the consciousness of the difference between what is and what ought to be, but in the clear knowledge that the divine unity of what is and what should be, that lives in him by grace, must be maintained in his life.

This is the conception that lies at the basis of the whole ethic of the gospels, of Paul and John. It means that we have not first to strive for the unity of what is and what should be, for it is already realized in God; that we have received a participation in this process, and that it *must* be unquestioningly realized in us. This obligation, since it is grounded on a divine necessity, requires the most complete commitment of the whole person, the application of all his powers. The demands it makes are so pressing that, in comparison, the categorical imperative of natural ethics is but a feeble summons. Thus Paul argues in Rom 6: since we *are* already dead with Christ, we cannot, should not conduct ourselves as if we were still living as before. Thus John in his letters, when he brings out the fundamental obligation of Christians: "In this we have known the charity of God, because he has laid down his life for us, and we *ought* to lay down our lives for the brethren"; "If God has so loved us, we also *ought* to love one another"; "This commandment we have from God, that he who loves God love also his brother." This necessity arises from the gift already implanted in us by God of his own identity, and so is not just an intensification of the claims of natural ethics. The urgency of its demands is not the product of a necessity indwelling in human nature, but of something placed there by God, at a deeper level than any reality of our own. It is something that lays claim to our whole being and, by that very fact, imposes an inescapable obligation.

The natural life can only be, like eros in Plato's conception, a life of want and of attempts to satisfy it. It strives ceaselessly and insatiably to fullness of being, and its nearest approach to this is the actual effort involved. The Christian life, the life of grace, of faith and charity, is necessarily one

31

that proceeds from fullness of being, and is, therefore, a life of thanksgiving: *eucharistia*. Enriched, beyond all hope and beyond all satisfaction of its indigence, from the abundant riches of eternal life, it can but be a continuous testimony to the gifts of grace. So it was that the psalmist lived in uninterrupted praise of God's mercy, and that Mary sang her Magnificat. So it is that the Christian, to whom eternal life has been given in faith and charity, has only to let himself be led by the current of this life so as to become himself wholly an expression of it. Consequently, in the Christian life, there are no "stages of development" in the sense of the ascetic and mystical "degrees" in the schemes of other religions. The only stages are those of the development of the life of grace in us, the ever more complete elimination of what blocks the way of grace. The Christian may, and must, constantly connect up with the riches already at hand, laid down in advance, and the more he does so and acts accordingly, the better Christian will he be. To take an already present perfection in the natural sphere for granted, or an end already attained, in this way, would be quite absurd, the kind of thing a beginner might do who wants to play the master. But for the Christian to refuse to set out from this fullness as his starting point would be equivalent to unbelief. The apostles were constantly at pains to rid ordinary Christians of this kind of unbelief, to encourage their faith to a complete reversal of standpoint, to make them conduct their lives from a point which they had only hoped to reach by Christian living. The more thorough the change of perspective, and the more fearless the leap, the easier it becomes. And those who try to follow the two ways at once—that of faith which starts with Christ, and that of man's indigence going to the Absolute—get caught up in an inextricable tangle. There is no common measure between nature and grace, reason and faith; only the order grounded in the person of Christ: nature as the expression and servant of the supernatural. In this service it will not be found wanting.

To understand the divine life of grace in us, it is essential not to revert to the view that the infusion of the theological virtues means in some sense or other that they are acquired. Faith and love, with which hope is conjoined, are to be understood primarily as the expression of the eternal life communicated to man; as something in consequence, far beyond the possibilities of the natural intelligence and will, for they spring immediately from the inmost life of the Trinity. Faith and charity, as understood by the gospels, are inseparable in this life. Faith is the surrender of one's own views, and can be permanent only as the outcome of love and fidelity. It means preferring the divine truth before one's own truth, because God is what he is. Faith is the intellect's love for God. According to Thomas, love is the principle of all merit (I, II, 114, 4), ultimately also of the merit of faith, of its obscurity, of the renunciation it entails. Love itself is the surrender of one's entire will and being through faith, in the conviction that God merits to be placed first in every respect and is deserving of total surrender; in a trust, too, that in its knowledge surpasses all knowledge. And it is precisely in this infinite surrender and self-renunciation, in this absolute preference of the Thou to the I, that the life of the Trinity consists; for it is a life in which the Persons can be conceived only "relatively," that is, through one another. The Father only is, as he who generates the Son, he who surrenders and pours himself out in the Son; and the Son is, only as he who utterly surrenders

33

himself to the Father, acknowledging himself to be the Father's glory and image; the Spirit is, only as witnessing and expressing the love between the Father and the Son, and proceeding from them. "Faith" and love are, in this sense, the core of the divine being and life, though faith, as here understood, includes all vision and knowledge, and therefore is taken in its analogous sense. Nonetheless, since eternal life, in order to be life, transcends itself to infinity, this "faith" cannot be a knowledge in any way restricted in scope; any limitation would cause this life and interchange of love to weaken and grow cold. But the supreme excellence of the eternal life does not exclude its capability of being present in various degrees. The faith and love by which man in grace lives comes from the infinity of the eternal life. If we confine ourselves to analyzing them as psychological acts, we leave out of account their inmost essence. Indeed they are psychological acts, but not acts of the old I, which "dies daily," but of that mysterious new I, which is only accessible through faith and love. The "natural" man directs his thought by the light of reason into the darkness of mystery; the Christian thinks in the light of the mystery of faith, by which he illuminates the darkness of the world.

2

At the core of created being is the tension between essence and existence, which is the basis of the category *ens commune*. On another level, though closely connected with the first, it is characterized by the tension between the universal and the particular, the abstract and the concrete. For there is no particular that is not the particularizing of a universal, the concretizing of an abstract, that cannot be subsumed under a more general category; nor, however, is there any universal which cannot be represented in a particular. For this reason, each pole presupposes the other, and elucidates the other. What has never been met before loses its strangeness, once it can be incorporated in something already known, and the bare universal takes on coloring when we can recall a concrete example. The confusion of the mass of individual things is cleared up by their assignment to various species, from which they derive unity, nature and law, and the species themselves, in which all individuality seems to vanish, receive an identity, a history and a significance from the undeniable character of what exists here and now. Intellect and sense, knowledge of the universal and view of the particular, condition one another, for the being of the world is so constituted as to correspond to this polarity, and so to reflect the divine unity in the mutual tension and irreducibility of generic and individual unity. This is why human thought, philosophy, oscillates between two impossible ideologies, realism and nominalism. The truth lies between the two, though never finally established, just as being itself lies somewhere between the universal and the particular. Likewise human religion and mysticism may seek to dissolve individuality in the purely universal, or to escape the curse of the collective that reduces all to the same level, in order to engage itself with the purely individual; but both these attempts at evasion are held up by the reality of being and what it comprises. No individual can be, as such, universal, and no universal individual.

But here also the two are identical in God, and, in the incarnation of Christ, God is brought into the world. Christ is neither one individual among others, since he is God and so not susceptible of comparison, nor is he the norm in the

35

sense of a universal, since he is this individual. Because he is God, he is a *Universale concretum,* a *Concretum universale.* It is for this reason that he is outside our most elementary modes of thought. He cannot, under any aspect, be classified. Neither in his particular nor in his universal aspect can he enter into comparison with any other. In philosophy it is true to say that the phoenix, an individual that in itself exhausts the species, is a contradiction, an impossibility. Theology, on the contrary, starts out from Christ who, as this individual, is universal, because embodying the absolute norm, and who, as this contingent being within history, is the necessary being above all history and nature; he it is to whom, as head, all things in heaven and earth must be brought back. He is indeed a man, and yet not an individual among others, since what distinguishes one man from another, the person, is in his case God. And he is, on the other hand, "the meaning of the Law," the supreme norm; yet he does not share the essential property of all secular laws and norms, that of being separable from the individual case. Consequently neither nominalism not extreme realism is applicable to him; and it would be a mistake to imagine that, in proceeding from the abstractness of the early medieval realism to the supposed concreteness of the later nominalism, one can get closer to the essence of Christianity. The uniqueness of Christ consists in this, that God came into the world in him alone, and no process of abstraction, no reduction to universal principles is of any avail for an understanding of this unity. This is the "nominalistic" side of Christianity. At the same time, Christ is the divine Logos in the world, who is himself the measure and rule for all abstract law and every concrete event. This is the "realistic," "Platonist" side of Christianity, and also the

36

"Aristotelian" side, the maintenance of the rights of sense over against pure reason. "That which we have heard, which we have seen with our eyes and our hands have handled, of the word of life . . ." This uniqueness of Christ, which everything in this world, both singular and general, depends on is the manifestation within creation of the uniqueness of God. God is not only one, he is the One, the Unique. Every creature has something of his uniqueness, but only in the setting of the greater dissimilarity arising from the tension between the general and the individual, which even the created spirit does not wholly escape. But in Christ the spirit is a divine person and, in its quality of person, is inseparable from the personal community of the Trinity. This community is not generic; it is what is most singular, but it is this precisely as community. It is an identity that wholly surpasses our imagining, as does the way in which the creaturely nonidentity between I and We is enriched beyond measure in the eternal ground wherein we are united through the uniqueness of Christ.

This uniqueness of Christ, being the uniqueness of God, in no way pertains to the world or is explicable in terms of the world, or comprehensible to it. Yet he lets us participate in it, giving it to his body, which is also his bride, the Church. He gives it, within this body, to his members, who, marked with the signs of his uniqueness, are visible to the world, at least negatively, as what "is not of this world." The world must, therefore, hate Christians, because it hates Christ, and, hating him, hates the Father (Jn 15:18ff). Now we cannot subsume God under any general concept, not even that of being, for this is essentially analogous, that is, its universality is not adequate to raise it in any relationship whatever above God, not even a logical one. Consequently it

37

is impossible to infer, from the uniqueness of God, the least thing that would not be the outcome of God's free self-revelation; nor can anything that directly depends on our participation through grace in God be subsumed under any of the categories of this world. We may perhaps, for the sake of logical convenience, apply the concept of *"societas perfecta"* both to the Church and the state, but such an application has no validity in the ontological order. The body of Christ, its presence by grace among men, is not only on quite a different level of being from that of the state, but, by its very uniqueness, is not amenable to any subsumption in the real order.

Christian thought, therefore, is radically different from the purely natural mode of thinking, which always proceeds by way of classification. Nothing that has to do with God's supernatural working out of salvation in the world is capable of classification. Certainly each event in it points to the uniqueness of God ever anew encountering us. With each event it manifests itself more, and we are caught up further into it; but this does not mean that it becames more familiar to us, as a subject becomes more familiar as we work at it. One can dominate a subject by mastering its general laws and grasping their application to individual cases. But from the thousands of events of the Old Testament it is impossible to construct a single a priori theory as to how God could or must have revealed himself in addition to them. We can come to know God, his works, his mind, his wisdom as revealed to us through his grace. We can learn better to understand the meaning of his present and future acts through his past ones, and the whole economy of salvation, with its teachings and prophecies, its constantly renewed applications, all the promises it contains and their fulfill-

38

ments, spurs us on toward this understanding. Yet with all this abundance of spiritual riches given to us by God, we are not entitled to deduce laws by which we could master the process of salvation and God's working. We can only understand this process in the measure we are willing to hear right to the end, and to involve ourselves wholly in the drama, insofar, therefore, as personal faith and self-giving love remain the foundation and summit of all our knowledge, for faith and love are a participation in the divine love, and the God of grace is not to be known without the God of grace. Christian knowledge, therefore, advances not so much in breadth—new truth is not attained by the application of logic—as in depth, in that faith reaches through the apparent finiteness of the words and acts which constitute revelation to the infinite abyss of the divine wisdom therein contained. Certainly this depth is itself capable of verbal expression, since it is a depth of the Word, and so theology is possible. But in theology the divine content is not expanded and explored on the level of the human mind, but rather the human mind is raised up and carried along in the mysterious dimension of God's own self-revelation.

3

The being of the world is in a state of tension between essence and existence, between the generic and the individual. But a being that is spiritual knows this is its structure, which is essentially one of movement and unrest. It is a structure that has no permanence in itself, and so is a standing proof of its contingency and creatureliness. And as a creature and a nature, the being subject to this tension is drawn in all its fibres back to the abyss from which it

originated and in which its dynamism is appeased, that is, in
the absolute identity of God, in the pure Being, beyond all
distinction of essence and existence, in the pure One, beyond
all division of generic and individual unity. From this it is
easy to see how all natural religion, mysticism and philosophy must envisage our relationship with God. On the
assumption that God had not revealed himself otherwise
than in the constitution of created being, creation alone
would have to serve as a guide to him. Everything in it
bears his trace, each essence as well as each existence, each
universal as well as each particular. Each element presents
itself as relevant here, and is so presented also by its counter-
part. The idea that God, as creator, has no sort of relation
to what he created, and that this expresses nothing of his
thought, and therefore of his being, is absurd. And yet a
cleavage runs through the very heart of the creature. There
is within it no hidden sphere of identity, no place where it
may venture to assert its existence as necessary, its individuality as of universal application. Consequently it knows
its poles only as relative, the one only through the other,
only for the sake of the other, and both so involved in the
relationship that, apart from it, they could not be assigned
any intelligible content at all. This relativity reveals itself
progressively; it increases the deeper man penetrates in
thought and experience. Everything that he and the world is
bears traces of God, but, in the end, it never manifests him.
There is a certain similarity, but it dissolves in an ever
greater dissimilarity. Everything points to God, but he is the
Wholly Other, the Unknown. And he is most unknown when
he transcends even the name of the Wholly Other, and becomes the Not Other (*Non aliud*). There is a *via affirma-
tiva*, but it issues in the *via negativa*, in which we know and

40

reverence God more profoundly, because we set aside all statements about him that do not describe him as he is. There cannot really be a third course, at all events not as a kind of synthesis of the two, in which knowledge by analogy—similarity in even greater dissimilarity—may be surpassed. It will be either the expression of the creature's continued aspirations, ever unsatisfied, or else of the fact that God has revealed himself in a degree far beyond the possibilities of nature.

Revelation, however, does not begin at the point where man might have expected it. It does not come about when he has passed through all that is relative in order to attain the absolute, when by a supreme effort he attempts to put his humanity behind himself in order to attain to some intimation of the divine. Natural mysticism and philosophy necessarily travel along this path, the way of negation and supersession of self; but it only knows the abstract opposition between relative and absolute, and can only attain the absolute in constantly transcending all that is relative. It must travel the way of "ascent," the way of the Platonist eros, seeking, by ridding itself by "degrees," of all that confines it, to become free of all barriers and, departing in the night, like a thief, from the house of its finitude, to enter that of infinity. What characterizes all mysticism and religious philosophy outside Christianity is—with all its delight in the senses—a distinct tendency to do away with becoming, to merge all that is finite in the abyss of the infinite God, to sink all definite words and ideas into the aboriginal ground of σιγή, of silence. Chinese and Indians, Greeks and Arabians, Plotinus, Eriugena and Böhme, Schelling and Rilke all agree in this. Christianity alone takes an optimistic course. The Word has become flesh. God has shown himself not on the farthest boundary of the world, but in its midst, indeed in its lowliest part. And since he prepared himself a body within the sphere of the finite, man does not draw near to him by denying all that limits him. A movement of ascent to God leaving the world behind was only justified as long as God had not descended, not revealed himself in a human body, in human words. (But that means never.) Any such attempt at ascent is not merely made less necessary, it is wholly superseded by God's descent to man. Man had, understandably enough, tried to forge a way for himself, but God shows another way. And it is not for man to try and combine the two or even to incorporate God's way into his own. There is no call for him to tax as heretical the attempt to forge a way to God. So long as no better course offers itself, one must make do with what one has; and if God does not put forth his hand, man must use his own powers to reach out to God. This is perfectly in order—or rather, would be, if God had not revealed himself from the very outset.

God's action in revealing himself makes an end of the mainly negative theology, in the sense in which the natural man must necessarily understand it. God is primarily a known God, a God who has disclosed himself, has shown who he is, and who has sent into us his Spirit, the very Spirit who searches the deep things of God and makes them known to us. We see the Son, and in him the Father, in faith now, in vision later. But faith and vision are so near each other, promise and fulfillment are so conjoined, that we already believe as if we saw, for we love the Son, who sees the Father; and we love the brethren in the love with which the Father and Son love one another; and, in so loving, we know what

God is. And the man, Christ, is not only a creature separated from the Creator by the abyss of his creatureliness. He is the begotten Son of the Father, and his created nature is drawn into the eternal act of generation. This nature is indeed entirely the expression and property of his divine person, so that everything that pertains to it is God's word and seal. "What we have heard, what we have seen with our eyes, and our hands have handled, of the word of life . . ." In Christ, but in him only, and yet, through him, in all that he includes in his sphere of grace; in Christ, in the Church, in the world, which, in its entirety, he came to redeem, created being, with its inner tensions, is made to speak of eternal life. The inaccessible summit of "absolute being" thaws, and from it streams forth the water of a life that is infinite. This life chooses as its vessel the life of the creature who, through the grace of the incarnation, is made capable of containing it. The relativity which belongs to the essence of created life no longer points only momentarily to God, and then becomes powerless to show us the Absolute. On the contrary, in Christ the human is so completely subjected to the divine and made its vessel that it can be made a lasting expression of eternal life. Each word, movement, look and gesture of the Lord is a revelation of eternal life; but equally so is his suffering, his darkness, his dereliction, his descent into hell. All this is God making himself known to man.

Everything in the created order, with the exception of sin, is enabled, through Christ, to be an expression of God, most of all what we would think to be most remote from him: the cross, opprobrium, anguish, death. And since the eternal life has made use of the whole range of the world's tensions to reveal its still wider range, man for his part must not

43

restrict himself to anything less in framing his idea of God. No longer may he conceive God as the transcendent apex of certain selected powers belonging to the creature; rather he must be capable now, for the first time, of really finding God in all things. In other words, he may not set aside all the potentialities of the creature so as to apprehend God as "pure act," but must see them all as the vessel and expression of the eternal activity of the eternal life; he must envisage the absolute life of God as beyond what we are wont to distinguish in the world as "act" and "potentiality." Through the Word of God, which is Christ, the whole world, in association with his taking flesh, begins itself to be God's body and word. God remains, even in his revelation, incomprehensible, beyond all our conception; but the access to him we are granted is no longer, as in the *theologia negativa,* a banishment to what is alien, inaccessible, dark; it means our being flooded with light, excess of light. God is love, and we can know this love and live by it; but it is in itself beyond our comprehension, flowing out superabundantly, the object of our adoration. We plunge deeper into it, and it inundates us. The more we live by it, the more we are truly ourselves. It makes us humble, for besides being absolute glory, it is also absolute humility. In the abyss of divine love we are ever more profoundly united without confusion, for in God himself the three persons celebrate, without confusion of being, the highest of unions.

4

It should now be clear how the Christian approach differs from the natural, and also in what sense it incorporates and completes the latter, instead of invalidating it. It does so

not by some vague synthesis of nature and the supernatural
—no synthesis of nature and God is possible—giving rise
to some kind of third approach embodying the two. Ultimately there is only one synthesis in which God has established his relationship to the world, namely Christ, the
incarnate Word of the Father. He is the measure of nearness
and distance from God; he is the *analogia entis* in concrete
form, he is the event that took place once and for all, and
at the same time the norm for all that is in the world. He
has truly descended, has taken man's nature from an already
existing humanity; but it is in virtue of this that he alone is
the standard by which God finally assesses the merit of all
that pertains to man. It is through this man that God looks
on each individual and estimates his worth. God looks on
him as the Head, and on the Church and the world as his
body and bride.

Nature, then, is perfected by being made the vessel and
expression of the divine. It gives itself over to become this
expression. It lets what is most ungodly in it be gathered in
by God, whose pleasure it is to make what is alien his own,
to make of the alogical the Logos, to be in the becoming
Being, in death superabundant life. Humility can go no
further, just as the Son is God in that he has the humility
to wish nothing else than to be the Word and image of the
Father. Nature, then, is perfected in that it consents to give up
trying to understand itself by considering its own problems
of being and obligation, of universality and particularity,
and instead starts from the fact of the divine life, which it is
not, but which it wills to live in and to make of it its exclusive dwelling. It is perfected in that it interprets itself not
by taking account of what it has by inheritance and acquisi-
tion, but on the more fundamental basis of what has been

45

divinely infused. In the sight of God, man is one whom Christ has redeemed, who has received from him the love that is God's, and, in that love, loves his brethren. Whatever else man may be is subordinate to this definition.

This is the idea of man in the mind of God, and to it the whole of nature is ordered as the seed to the flower. It cannot be said that nature is diminished by being held to serve as a vessel for the divine. What act of the human will could be more sublime than that of divine love? What could be more sublime for the human understanding than to elicit the act of divine faith? The whole problem of finite being, seen in this context, is resolved. The tension in finite being between what it is and what it ought to be is not eliminated; the movement is not brought to a halt, but starts out afresh from a new point and under new conditions, namely from the fact of the life divinely infused; and it makes use of this fact for its purposes. Neither are human modes of thinking and argument to be rejected as no longer necessary, for the Word of God has expressed itself in human words and concepts, and human speech and thought can be used by it further to bring out all its divine riches. The reflections of Paul and John show how legitimate such a procedure is—so legitimate, in fact, that in their case it forms part of revelation. The gold of the Egyptians was only of value when it came into the hands of the Israelites; and reason is only serviceable to faith when it takes on the form of faith. We cannot attempt to blend, in our premises, the truth of revelation and that of pure nature, and squeeze out thereby a hybrid conclusion. Everything must be drawn into the setting of faith; all natural premises must be taken in the sense of faith, and so made capable of wider application. At the same time, the content of faith will itself constantly come to include more than reason apprehends; and it is just when the logical process is correct that there is present in the conclusion something of the unknown mystery that was latent in one or both of the premises.

The content of revelation is always infinite, and infinitely overflows the finite vessel into which it is poured, however authentic the vessel. For example, the identity of what is and what ought to be, which is the form of God and is yet present also in the background of the grace given, remains God's and cannot be, as a fact finally accomplished, something of man. Though he knows himself to be a child of God, he must, on that account, strive no less hard with his human powers, not only with this identity as a starting point, but also as his aim, since it can always be intensified, always exceed present attainment. There are certain conclusions it is not permitted to him to draw from the fact of the identity accorded him. For example, he is not to rest content with the knowledge that grace is an infused gift, as though it did not also depend on him, or—a temptation often alluded to by Paul as extremely dangerous—sin, in order that grace may abound the more. Even were this true of grace, one may not do so. There are, then, certain limits drawn—in fact, many apply to beginners, but not to the "advanced," "those fit for strong meat"—but this is not because the divine cannot insert itself in a human vessel, but because it is itself so human, and we bear the glory of God in earthen vessels. The divine gift of participation penetrates the inmost being of the creature, and so brings it to fulfillment together with all its strivings, which, without grace, would remain nugatory, since the creature's perfecting depends not on its own potentialities, but on the power of God. The infusion of the divine identity does not involve any strain or distortion of the creature's potential, for it takes place through God's own condescension and abasement to the forms of creaturely nonidentity. Nor does participation in the divine uniqueness do violence to what is nameless, specific in the creature, since God himself, in Christ, is "Son of man," one man, that is, among all the rest; and further, because he himself stoops down, in the eucharistic species, to matter which is nameless and formless. Nor in the positive ordinances of the loving God does he oppress us with his love, but in his lowliness he always remains infinitely above us, in his nearness he is yet distant, though known he is still the Unknown to whom the Son, dying, called out in his darkness. Thus the forms and categories of philosophy and mysticism are not simply sundered; instead they have to be judged according to whether they convey the spirit of Christianity or some other spirit. Often the disparity is great and evident. Often it is slight, and then the Christian soul can only be known through a certain barely perceptible fragrance, as for instance that of the Areopagite in Neoplatonism. In the same way, the originality of a work of art cannot be perceived through the application of general rules, nor by some accidental quality, but by the impression it gives of complete inevitability with perfect freedom, overwhelming the beholder, and making him say: it could only have been thus.

THEOLOGY AND SANCTITY

1. UNITY AND DIVISION

In the whole history of Catholic theology there is hardly anything that is less noticed, yet more deserving of notice, than the fact that, since the great period of scholasticism, there have been few theologians who were saints. We mean here by theologian one whose office and vocation is to expound revelation in its fullness, and therefore whose work centers on dogmatic theology. If we consider the history of theology up to the time of the great scholastics, we are struck by the fact that the great saints, those who not only achieved an exemplary purity of life, but who also had received from God a definite mission in the Church, were, mostly, great theologians. They were "pillars of the Church," by vocation channels of her life: their own lives reproduced the fullness of the Church's teaching, and their teaching the fullness of the Church's life.

This is the reason for their enduring influence: the faithful saw in their lives an immediate expression of their teaching and a testimony to its value, and so were made fully confident in the rightness of teaching and acting. It also gave the teachers themselves the full assurance that

49

they were not deviating from the canon of revealed truth; for the complete concept of truth, which the gospel offers us, consists precisely in this living exposition of theory in practice and of knowledge carried into action. "If you continue in my word . . . you shall know the truth" (Jn 8:32). "He that seeks the glory of him that sent me, he is true, and there is no injustice in him" (Jn 7:18). And even stronger: "He who says that he knows him, and keeps not his commandments, is a liar, and the truth is not in him" (1 Jn 2:4). "He that loves not knows not God, for God is charity" (1 Jn 4:8).

From the standpoint of revelation, there is simply no real truth which does not have to be incarnated in an act or in some action, so that the incarnation of Christ is the criterion of all real truth (1 Jn 2:22; 4:2), and "walking in the truth" is the way the believer possesses the truth (2 Jn 1–4; 3 Jn 3–4, etc.). Since the Holy Spirit distributes offices in the Church according to his will, and gives to some the grace to be "teachers" (Eph 4:11; 1 Cor 12:29), for which he imparts the gift of "knowledge in the Spirit" (1 Cor 12:8), the office of teacher will consist in proclaiming and transmitting the truth of revelation, manifested in the life of Christ, in such a way that the hearer can recognize it through his "walking in the truth" and can thus verify it. For Christ, the exemplar of the truth, who designates himself as the truth, is for us the canon of truth only in that his existence manifests his essence, which is to be the "image of God" (2 Cor 4:4). "I do always the things that please him" (Jn 8:29).

It was by virtue of this unity of knowledge and life that the great teachers of the Church were able, as was required by their special office, to be true lights and pastors of the Church. For although the pastoral office is numbered by Paul in association with that of teacher (Eph 4:11), this does not mean that all pastors must be teachers, though their office involves their sharing the work of transmitting doctrine (2 Tim 2:24, etc.). Likewise, the great teachers are not necessarily pastors, though, even if they are not bishops, they participate in the pastoral office. It is not surprising, therefore, to find that, in the early centuries, the offices of teacher and of pastor (in the sense of Eph 4 and 1 Cor 12) were normally conjoined. Irenaeus, Cyprian, Athanasius, the two Cyrils, Basil, Gregory of Nazianzen, Gregory of Nyssa, Epiphanius, Theodore of Mopsuesta, Chrysostom, Theodoret, Hilary, Ambrose, Augustine, Fulgentius, Isidore—all were bishops, not to mention the two great popes, Leo and Gregory. Among the great doctors, exceptions to this rule were the two Alexandrians, Jerome, Maximus and John of Damascus; but these representatives of the monastic and ascetical life bring out still more clearly the union of doctrine and life. The same may be said, too, of most of the bishops and teachers mentioned above, who were either monks themselves or were closely associated with monasticism and promoters of it.

In short, these pillars of the Church were complete personalities: what they taught they lived with such directness, so naively, we might say, that the subsequent separation of theology and spirituality was quite unknown to them. It would not only be idle but contrary to the very conceptions of the fathers to attempt to divide their works into those dealing with doctrine and those concerned with the Christian life (spirituality). It is true that they wrote works of

51

controversy and apologetics; but these, fundamentally, do not constitute a distinct branch, but served, at the time they appeared, as a spur to the development of doctrine. When Irenaeus, Basil, Gregory of Nazianzen or Augustine argue with their adversaries, they do not operate in a forecourt of theology, but in its very center. The answers they give express the fullness and depth of revelation in its central teaching. When they speak of those "outside," their attitude is the same as when they speak of those within, though to the former they may have to explain certain things that are clear enough to the latter. And when they explain the Christian life to those within, it is always and exclusively in the form of an exposition of traditional doctrine. One might perhaps allow a distinction between the commentaries and homilies of Origen, the former being more speculative and the latter more pastoral in interest; but if we look deeper, the distinction vanishes; in both, Origen is concerned with expounding the word of God, which is as much a word of life as a word of truth. One could, of course, list a number of the works—chiefly shorter ones—of the fathers as being more practical in scope, which could be classified under the heading "spirituality"; but, just as their works of controversy are, at the same time, doctrinal and theological, so too are those which treat of the Christian life.

This notion of "theology and sanctity" is illuminatingly corroborated and, as it were, canonized by that mysterious writer who, next to Augustine, did most to form the theology of the middle ages, and even of modern theology, namely the Areopagite. His *Ecclesiastical Hierarchy* (to which the *Celestial Hierarchy* forms little more than an "ideological superstructure") is framed throughout on an a priori (which has become for us almost inconceivable) identification of hierarchical office and personal holiness. Denis was a far too superior mind for us to impute this action to a naive ignorance of the world; in any case, we have the witness of many of his letters, especially the celebrated one to Demophilus, which shows he was fully alive to the actual defects in the Church. But Denis was of the opinion that we can only grasp the structure of the Church and make it intelligible if we start from what *ought* to be, what, in fact *is,* when seen in its existence in Christ and in its direct constitution by Christ. The degrees in the hierarchy *must,* therefore, be put on an identical footing with the degrees of inner purification, illumination and unification; to understand what the episcopal office *really* is, we must think of it as embodied in one who has reached perfection, who possesses the fullness of contemplation, the highest degree of initiation into the mysteries of God. In the above-mentioned letter, Denis does not shrink from the conclusion that only one who is himself a "light of the world" can communicate what is sacred, can illuminate. We are inclined to see, in this, the Donatist error, and not to take sufficient account of the constant basic principle of his vision of the Church. Denis, in fact, is not thinking of any purely subjective perfection, but of the gospel image of perfection. And if any commentary is needed, one only has to turn to Lallemant's invective against priests and religious who, ignoring the Holy Spirit and vegetating at the lowest stages of the Christian life, are powerless to communicate the Spirit to others. Up to the time of Thomas, Denis' concept of the structure of the Church and the hierarchy was the pattern, though often after Thomas' time the clarifying distinction between *status perfectionis* and actual perfection (II, II, 184, 4), and his sober estimate of the relations between the episcopal and religious states (185, 3–8) were bound to come in. It is through the writings of Denis that the *de jure* identification of bishop, saint and teacher of the Church was most effectively impressed on theology, and this has been received as part of the gospel tradition.

The early medieval thinkers in the west, under the aegis of Augustine, did not depart from this basic concept. Anselm, himself abbot, bishop and doctor of the Church, knew no other canon of truth than the unity of knowledge and life. The same may be said of Bede, Bernard and Peter Damian. But as theology increasingly took on a "scholastic" form, and Aristotelianism burst in like an elemental force, the naive unity hitherto accepted was gravely shaken. No one would think of denying that the gain in clarity, insight and mastery of the entire field was enormous. More resoundingly than in the time of the fathers, who, almost as a matter of course, achieved eminence in the schools of antiquity, was the jubilation over the *spolia Aegyptiorum* repeated. The mood which fastened on Christian thinkers was like the intoxication of victors after a battle, at the sight of booty far beyond their expectations.

The booty in this case, however, was primarily philosophical, and only indirectly theological. Philosophy began to emerge as a special discipline alongside theology, with its own concept of philosophical truth, which was perfectly correct in its own sphere, and could lay no claim to the superior content of revealed truth. *Adaequatio intellectus ad rem:* this definition envisaged, primarily, only the theoretical side of truth. The intimate connection was seen, and indeed emphasized, between the true and the good as the transcendental properties of the one being, but it was looked at more from the human standpoint, in the mutual presupposition of intellect and will (S. Th. I, 16,4 and ad 2), than in their objective mutual inclusion, or real identity. Philosophy, as a doctrine of natural being and excluding revelation, could not know that the highest mode of interpreting that philosophical definition of truth must be a trinitarian one, corresponding to the passages on truth in St. John already cited. There was no danger of misconceiving supernatural truth, so long as philosophical concepts were used as pointers to the final truth which is supernatural and divine. These concepts, in being taken up as part of the *assumptio humanae naturae* in Christ, lost nothing of their content—just as Christ's humanity in its entirety subsisted in the Logos—but yet, through this assumption, they must be, as Scheeben says, "transfigured," and become, like Christ's humanity, wholly a function and expression of his divine person and truth.

But the Aristotelianism of the thirteenth century did not only enlarge the basis of theology, it was itself the start of the modern sciences of nature and mind as independent disciplines, and rightly so. It gave birth to modern "secularism," and thereby introduced new tensions and set new problems to the Christian. The great scholastic period of Albert, Bonaventure and Thomas was peculiarly fitted for theology to irradiate and transfigure the self-subsisting science of nature, raising it to the plane of the sacred, and so to impart to the secular sciences a real Christian ethos, one affecting the whole outlook of the scientific investigator.

55

But the work of transposing the concepts and methods of the physical and mental sciences, and articulating them with theology, was bound to become more and more difficult, and post-scholastic theology rarely applied itself to the task (in their own way, Nicholas of Cusa, Leibniz and Baader did, but they were not taken up into official theology). For the most part, it confined itself to using a natural theology, antecedent to biblical theology, as a basis for a rational exposition of the latter. Moreover this was not without its dangers, especially when the philosophical propaedeutic came to be considered a fixed and unalterable basis, whose concepts, without the necessary transposition, were used as norms and criteria of the content of faith, and therefore set in judgment over it. Teachers behaved as though man knew from the outset, before he had been given revelation, knew with some sort of finality what truth, goodness, being, light, love and faith were. It was as though divine revelation on these realities had to accommodate itself to these fixed philosophical conceptual containers that admitted of no expansion. Nor was the actual method of teaching calculated to lessen the danger. On the contrary, the student was, first of all, required to familiarize himself with the concepts of philosophy and their content, before going on to their application in theology; and he needed an almost superhuman vigilance not to approach theology with preconceived concepts which needed to be "strained" to the utmost. If those established on natural grounds were to be raised to a higher plane and seen in the light of biblical revelation, that was no task for the beginner; it needed the highest degree of maturity, of genius allied with holiness. Albert, Bonaventure, Thomas, perhaps even Scotus, achieved the task. They did not allow their ultimate understanding of the truth to be disturbed by the fullness of the irruption of philosophical truth; and so the original conception of the teacher in the Church, who was by inner necessity a saint, could once again be embodied in them.

2. THE BURDEN OF THE DIVORCE BETWEEN THEOLOGY AND SANCTITY

The following epoch saw the disappearance of the "complete" theologian in the above sense, the theologian who is also a saint. In fact, spiritual men were turned away from a theology which was overlaid and overloaded with secular philosophy—with the result that alongside dogmatic theology, meaning always thereby the central science which consists in the exposition of revealed truth, there came into being a new science of the "Christian life," one derived from the mysticism of the middle ages and achieving independence in the *devotio moderna*. On this byway, of course, we continue to find saints. It is also true that, later, there were still teachers who were saints: John of the Cross was a doctor, not of dogmatic but of mystical theology; Canisius —certainly no theologian—was an interpreter of doctrine to ordinary people; Bellarmine a controversialist; Alphonsus a moralist. None of them centered his life, I do not say on dogma, but on dogmatic theology. This is true even of Francis of Sales who, as the founder of *spiritualité,* assured to it a recognized though never a clearly defined place among the ecclesiastical sciences.

Bremond, in his *Métaphysique des saints,* without intending it, laid his finger on this tender spot in modern theology.

What would the fathers of the Church have made of this as a title? Do the saints really need, really demand a special metaphysics all their own? And in what will this consist? In some kind of esoteric teaching about *oraison pure,* a teaching that ignores ordinary dogmatic theology or else soars far beyond it, into the empyrean heights of a sublime asceticism and mysticism? If this is so, it is hardly surprising that it gave rise to subtle differentiations of terminology, and to various controversies between a more ascetical and a more mystical approach, between Bossuet and Fénelon, Alvarez and Rodriguez, between the various representatives of a rarified *sentiment religieux*—all of which proceeded, for the most part, quite unconnected with any development in dogmatic theology. The mere fact that Bremond could write such a comprehensive *Histoire littéraire du sentiment religieux* without even having to mention the contemporary state of theology as the science of doctrine is one of the more alarming facts of recent Church history.

Bremond, however, did not invent that strange abstraction. He found it already in existence, and the saints themselves bear some of the responsibility. The first of these, perhaps, was the "backward" student of scholastic philosophy and theology in Alcala, Salamanca and Paris, whose scholastic studies left virtually no trace in his writings or on his life's work: Ignatius Loyola. The little book of the Exercises, which he bequeathed to his society as the basis of its holiness, contains, it is true, at the end a brief recommendation both of the scholastic and the positive methods in theology, an indication of the equal weight to be attached to the scholastics and the fathers—a most valuable prescription for all his disciples; but nothing in the substance

58

of the book is dependent, even by implication, on scholasticism. Ignatius draws his knowledge directly from revelation, with the combination of simplicity and prudence characteristic of the saints. It is a revelation coming with the same immediacy from scripture and the Church as from the inner illumination of the Spirit, especially from that overwhelming infusion of the Spirit given at the river Cardoner. There he received such prodigious light that, at the close of his life, he confessed that all God's help, all the knowledge he had been granted throughout his life, was not to be compared with what he then experienced. Both his ironical observations on the occasion of his encounter with the Dominicans and the Inquisition, when he was virtually equated with the illuminists and Erasmians, and still more the nominal notes he left on the matter, as well as the type of holiness envisaged by the Exercises, make it perfectly clear that there was one point on which he would not give an inch: the inner teaching of the Holy Spirit. Though he had not the slightest intention of inaugurating a "new theology" —for which he was conscious neither of the vocation nor the ability—he fastened on the Johannine idea of the identity of knowledge and life. The Exercises lead up to a "choice," arising from the fullness of the contemplation of the life of the Lord, a life springing up from the fullness of the Christian idea. This is what made them the basis for the chief school of sanctity for succeeding centuries. They simply restored the simple Christian conception of truth, which is the unity of knowledge and action. Just as Thomas became the patron of all Christian schools of theology, of whatever religious order, so the Ignatian Exercises became the practical school of holiness for all the orders.

But there was one thing Ignatius could not accomplish. He could not prevent the growing estrangment between theology and sanctity, any more than his pupils could. It is a remarkable fact and one worth noting that none of the numerous early commentators managed to transpose the special standpoint of the Exercises into a foundation for a system of dogmatic theology. This was due to various causes. Whether or not it was clearly enough perceived, it needed the insight of an Erich Przywara, of a Karl Rahner, of a Gaston Fessard, to extract and clarify it into a profound "theology of the Exercises"—though perhaps the baroque period was unfavorable to such an enterprise because of the excessive refinement and formalizing of its approach to the problems at hand, its theological rationalism, as shown by the inconclusive debate on predestination and free will. Furthermore dogmatic theology on the one hand and ascetical and mystical theology on the other were by then recognized and treated as independent and distinct subjects; and most theologians, in commenting on and teaching the Summa of Thomas, felt no call to reunite them. Many, indeed, were aware of something lacking; Denis Petau, Thomassin, the Maurists and other great editors attempted to restore unity by going back to the sources. Others worked at translating and furthering an understanding of the fathers. But there was no real endeavor in the direction of a living understanding of dogmatic theology.

Among the spirituals, those many who sought for an adequate expression of their understanding of revelation, of their contemplation and love of God, found the study of philosophy and theology one long penance. This was true not only of the less intellectually gifted, such as Vianney, but of Aloysius and John of the Cross. Some simply found food for their devotion in contemplating the gospel, without reference to their other studies. Others attempted, not always successfully, to make a synthesis between what it was their particular mission to proclaim and the traditional formulas of scholasticism; or, if they could not assimilate these in their whole range, or perhaps did not want to, they selected particular stones from the building to use as the substructure for their own personal teaching. This was how Francis of Sales, "Theotimus," came to formulate his teaching on love, the weakness of whose first theoretical part stands out by contrast with what follows, the soul's untrammeled ascent to God. More significant still is the *Ascent to Mount Carmel,* where the flight of the dove is impeded by the clumsy scholastic terminological armament—in fact, the dry, scarcely assimilated scholastic excerpts are John's own.

These two examples show only too clearly how matters then stood, and how the means of expression at the disposal of these two saints differed from those of Ephraem, Gregory of Nyssa or Augustine. The fathers found straightaway the appropriate dogmatic clothing for their very personal experience; everything became objective, and all the subjective conditions, experiences, fears, strivings, the "shock" in a word, were made to serve a fuller understanding of the content of revelation, to orchestrate its great themes. Every form of spirituality, of mysticism was seen as serving a function in the Church. Like sanctity itself, they were above all tasks within the Church. It had not yet been forgotten that Paul took all the subjective charismata, and, far from rejecting them or setting them aside, resolutely freed them from the dangers of subjectivism and reorientated them by

inserting them in the factual structure of the Church. It is
true that, even in those times, there were certain offshoots
which, if pursued, might have led to a spirituality independent of dogmatic theology—for example, Evagrius
Ponticus, the Messalianers and other sects who gave undue
prominence to religious experience—even the theology of
Evagrius, Macarius, or of Diadochus of Photike, or of
Cassian was more steeped in dogma than its counterparts
among the spiritual writers of the *grand siècle.*

The teaching of the latter was not, of course, in any way
in contradiction with dogmatic theology—Francis of Sales
and John of the Cross are, in fact, doctors of the Church—
but it is nonetheless true that it was, primarily, not a mysticism of service in the Church, but one of subjective experience, individual states. The mystical states are, of course, the
objects of John of the Cross' and Teresa of Avila's descrip-
tions; roughly speaking, the external objects are derived
from the state which reveals them. In this respect, Spanish
mysticism is in strong contrast with that of the Bible: from
the mysticism of the Apocalypse, where the seer, in ecstasy,
is wholly oblivious of himself in his office of transmitting the
revelations; from the mysticism of the patriarchs and
prophets; of Mary and Joseph, Paul and Peter, where the
inner graces all serve the single act of revelation. It is very
different, again, from the dogmatic mysticism of Hildegard
of Bingen, of Matilda, Bridget and the two Catherines, with
whom it was preeminently a question of serving the Church
in conveying an objective message, itself no other than an
interpretation of the one revelation for contemporary needs.
When the main emphasis is transposed to an inner experience, to its degrees, laws, sequences, variations, dog-

matic theology is relegated to the background. A close connection with the doctrinal teachings on God, the creation and the redemption ceases to be evident; whereas, often enough, the connections, parallels and analogies with religious phenomena outside Christianity are correspondingly more frequent and prominent.

Theology and spirituality have become, as it were, each a world of its own, with hardly any point of contact, and so the saints and spiritual writers are more and more ignored by theologians. What modern treatise of theology, which adduces as its highest authority, next to the Bible, the great saints of the patristic and scholastic ages, feels equally obliged to cite any of the three above-mentioned doctors, or to accord them equal weight, not to mention the numerous other later saints, such as John Vianney and Teresa of Lisieux? Where theology is concerned, they hardly exist; they are left for "spirituality" to plunder. And spirituality hardly exists any longer for theology. We have seen that the modern saints themselves are not without their share of responsibility for this state of affairs. They are not taken seriously in theology because they themselves did not venture to be theologically minded.

It is all very well to devote oneself to much thinking; but not all thinking is fruitful. One may make all sorts of deductions, but not every deduction is capable of being embodied in the Christian life. *Non plus sapere quam oportet sapere, sed sapere ad sobrietatem. Non alta sapientes, sed humilibus consentientes* (Rom 12:3, 16). The saints, intimidated by the conceptual entanglements drawn round the gospel truth, no longer dare to collaborate in the necessary work of exposition of doctrine, or think themselves qualified

63

to do so. They leave dogma to the prosaic work of the School, and become—lyrical poets. But just as poetry has developed from an objective art interpreting reality, the conception of Greeks and Romans, to a subjective art describing inner states, the expressionistic and impressionistic art of modern times, so also have the saints come to speak a religious language which is not dogmatic. Or else they obey instructions and respond to the demands made on them, which are more and more of a subjective and psychological nature. The saints in modern times are required to describe the way in which they experienced God, and the accent is always on experience rather than on God: for the nature of God is a subject for the theological specialist. Thus we see people such as Marie de l'Incarnation (by no means inferior to the great Teresa of Lisieux) straining to describe their mystical states. Teresa had herself set the example, urged on, of course, by her confessors. It is a fatal path to take, and ends up in the psychological laboratory, with its experiments and statistics—in other words, discrediting an ecclesial and charismatic witness, and degrading it to the status of a private utterance, which often gives every appearance of being satisfactorily grasped by ordinary worldly methods, very often sub-Christian. Has anyone worked out from the sanctity of the Curé of Ars all that his mission implies for the theology of confession? And if more had been demanded from Teresa of Lisieux than a pious account of her life, accommodated, moreover, to the taste of her own sisters, we might have learned even more astonishing things than she herself infiltrated throughout her pages.

Consider the doctrinal wealth drawn from the writings of

the Areopagite—not without reason the most commented on of all the mystics—in comparison with that yielded by even the greatest of the moderns, John of the Cross. And then compare, if you can bring yourself to do so, the nourishment offered by a modern theological manual for a life of holiness with that contained in any patristic commentary on scripture. The impoverishment brought about by the divorce between the two spheres is all too plain; it has sapped the vital force of the Church of today and the credibility of her preaching of eternal truth. This impoverishment is felt considerably more strongly by those who have to preach to the modern pagans than by professors in their seminary lecture rooms. It is the former who look round for some example of the conjunction of wisdom and holiness. They long to discover the living organism of the Church's doctrine, rather than a strange anatomical dissection: on the one hand, the bones without the flesh, "traditional theology"; on the other, the flesh without bones, that very pious literature that serves up a compound of asceticism, mysticism, spirituality and rhetoric, a porridge that, in the end, becomes indigestible through lack of substance. Only the two together (corresponding to the prototype of revelation in scripture) constitute the unique "form" capable of being "seen" in the light of faith by the believer, a unique testimony, invisible to the world, and a "scandal" to it.

A remedy for this state of things was sought, a few years ago, by a group of theologians who formulated what they called "kerygmatic theology." It took as its starting point two apparently certain facts: that it was impossible to repair the estrangement from life of traditional scholasticism, and that the contemporary preaching of revealed truth imperatively called for a new theoretical basis. Its solution, then, was to set up a new, unpretentious structure, chiefly concerned with the practical needs of pastoral work, and not forgetting that a very large number of theological students are intellectually quite incapable of coping with scholastic treatises. This was carried to the point of claiming to justify the twofold approach to theology on the ground of scholastic ontology itself, by resorting to the distinction between *verum* and *bonum:* scholasticism was held to have the *verum* as its primary object, kerygmatic theology the *bonum,* that is, the practical evaluation of revealed truth in view of the pastoral office.

This solution, carried to its conclusion, would mean perpetuating the mischievous cleavage in theology, and would be tantamount to declaring bankrupt the speculative power of reason enlightened by faith. The proposal follows the main trend of modern thought, the deepest theme of which is surely the divorce between spirit and life, between the theoretical and practical reason, between Apollo and Dionysos, idea and existence, between its conception of the spiritual world as valuable but impotent, and of the practical world as one of power but spiritual poverty. This dualism in philosophy has prevailed at least since Kant, and, in extreme form, is found in French and German existentialism. We need not inquire here whether it expresses the weariness and decadence of our culture, or if this defeatism of thought is a symptom of the pathological state of modern Europe; Christianity, about which theology is concerned, has no need to borrow its modes and movements of thought from those current in the secular world. Its very law of life raises it above the ebb and flow of secular culture; and one sign of this should be that it draws the remedy for its ills from its own store of supernatural strength.

3. Toward a New Unity

We cannot hope to recover this unity except by making a serious reassessment of the nature of theology. Once again, we mean by theology the central science of dogma, to the exclusion of every possible and justifiable preparatory study or subsidiary subject, everything in the nature of apologetics directed to the nonbeliever, all research, philological and historical, into the texts which transmit revelation to us; in other words, all the auxiliary sciences, whose direct concern is not the pure exposition of revelation from the standpoint of faith for those who believe. As a clearly defined subject, there are two aspects of dogmatic theology which call for reflection: its content and its form.

The content of dogmatic theology is revelation itself, which it aims to understand in a living faith, and to set forth by the application of reason animated and illuminated by faith and love. Dogmatic theology has its center precisely where revelation has its center, just as faith, the basic act on which rests the work of exposition, has its center at the very heart of revelation. Dogmatic theology is no mere connecting link between revelation and something else, such as human nature or reason or philosophy. Human nature and its mental faculties are given their true center when in Christ; in him they attain their final truth, for such was the will of God, the creator of nature, from eternity. Man, therefore, in investigating the relationship *between* nature and supernature, has no need to abandon the standpoint of faith,

67

to set himself up as the mediator between God and the world, between revelation and reason, or to cast himself in the role of judge *over* that relationship. All that is necessary is for him to understand "the one mediator between God and man, the man Christ Jesus" (1 Tim 2:5), and to believe him in whom "were all things created in heaven and on earth . . . all by him and in him" (Col 1:16). Christ did not leave the Father when he became man to bring all creation to fulfillment; and neither does the Christian need to leave his center in Christ in order to mediate him to the world, to understand his relation to the world, to build a bridge between revelation and nature, philosophy and theology.

The theologian has to bear the tension, so greatly heightened since the middle ages, between the revelation of Christ and secular science, including philosophy. But the gravity of the problem of being only really touches him at the point when it becomes transparent: as the relationship between God and the world, which in its most concrete form is that between Christ and the Church; for they are not only historical "facts," but the center of being in the process of self-realization (*actualitas essendi*).

This is what the saints are fully aware of. They never at any moment leave their center in Christ. They give themselves to their work in the world, while "praying at all times" and "doing all to the glory of God" (1 Tim 5:17; 1 Cor 10:31). When they philosophize, they do so as Christians, which means as believers, as theologians. In any case, all true philosophy outside Christianity is at bottom theology, since it lives and is kept alive by a point, a gravitational pull, external to itself, that mysterious Absolute that lies beyond the purview of merely human reason and

68

that alone makes thought worthwhile. How much truer then must this be of the great Christian thinkers: the more intense their sense of God and his holiness, the more fervent their language. And this simply means that their thought is a function of their faith; even though, as in Anselm's case, they may for the sake of understanding momentarily prescind from faith. Their thinking is an act that is ultimately performed in the service of their faith, of Christ's revelation, which is its norm and guiding principle.

A Christian thinker, when he truly thinks in theological terms, does not merely exercise himself in uncommitted disputation; he can let the value of his thought be measured by the revelation of Christ. Anything that really contributes to the elucidation of revelation, to bringing out its relevancy more forcefully in any way will not only be correct, but useful—true thought, in the deepest sense. Whatever leads away from the center of revelation, however logical the process, and draws attention to peripheral matters, or serves only human curiosity or vanity (and nothing is vainer than the human mind in its thinking) is part of the "knowledge that puffs up" (1 Cor 8:1). However correct logically, it is hollow and vain, nothing but wind. *Vanitas* is a theological category which may comprise any secular value, even those of the good and true in a secular sense, if the value is not directed on and informed by the supernatural values of faith and love.

True theology, the theology of the saints, with the central doctrines of revelation always in view, inquires, in a spirit of obedience and reverence, what processes of human thought, what modes of approach are best fitted to bring out the meaning of what has been revealed. That meaning does

69

not involve teaching anything occult or abstruse, but bringing men and their whole existence, intellectual as well as spiritual, into closer relation with God. Any intellectual procedure that does not serve this purpose is assuredly not an interpretation of revelation, but one that bypasses its true meaning and, therefore, an act of disobedience. Theology possesses in the form of revelation itself the unmistakable pattern for its own structure. Whatever is of substantial importance in revelation must receive corresponding prominence in theology. But what is only peripheral and is alluded to, as it were, merely in passing in revelation should only be treated incidentally in theology. In other words, the proportions of revelation should be those of theology. If it is to be a prolongation of the message of revelation, then the prolongation must be organically linked with its starting point, the central teaching of revelation; it should extend equally on all sides, and in that way respect the detailed structure of revelation, through a delicate sense of all its nuances.

As an example, let us consider the central point of revelation, namely the Trinity, from which all the rest proceeds, and to which all returns. The task of the first centuries of theology was to develop the doctrine on its main lines, and to protect it from elementary misconceptions; this was, on the whole, achieved by the time of Chalcedon. Augustine was the first to venture to probe beyond this first stage with his doctrine of the Image. In so doing, he disclosed a vast field for investigation, the whole mystery of being, as seen in the light of the revelation of the Trinity, begun in creation and carried further in Christ and the Church. From then on, the task would be to interpret the whole history of salvation, the life of Christ, the passion, the descent into hell, the resurrection and ascension, the Church and the Christian life, all in terms of the Trinity, as manifesting it. How rich the first biblical revelation of the Trinity is in this respect, namely the account of the annunciation! There we see, in the three stages of the dialogue with the angel, Mary (the believing Sion, and therefore the type of the Church) initiated into her own particular form of service: the Lord is with you, you shall bear a son (who will be called the Son of the Most High, and will rule the house of Jacob), the Holy Ghost will overshadow you (and behold, your cousin Elizabeth also . . .). Each successive revelation of the divine mystery is occasioned by a fresh demand on Mary and her assent to it: the Trinity emerges in the context of her obedience, her virginal state, and the New Testament contains no revelation of it that falls outside this context. Mary's attitude is, indeed, one of contemplation, but of a kind that is, at its source, one conjoined with the action of her loving response; it is a contemplation which "keeps all these things in her heart," only to bring forth what she has been given and contemplated and hand them on to the world. Likewise the gospels are the fruit of contemplation, brought forth from the womb of the primitive Church, and, for this reason, they cannot give us any other image of the Trinity than the marian one, that is to say, embodied in the actual life of these persons depicted in revelation, principally of the incarnate God himself, and explicable only in that context. This does not mean that deviations from the doctrine must not be countered by clear and distinct arguments, but that these serve merely to erect defenses and warning signs on the frontiers, while all that they can furnish in the interior is a few indications of a quite formal nature, within which, as a framework, the living experience of faith has to work out its own interpretation of itself. This experience is related primarily to what is revealed supernaturally rather than to revelation in nature (as is the case with Augustine's treatment in the second part of the *De Trinitate*), and so has less to do with an image than with the revelation of the archetype itself. It is quite possible that the image can be significant for the understanding of revelation, but more important is what it stands for.

An interpretation along these lines could have led to a specifically Christian doctrine of reality, to an explanation of existence and history in the light of revelation. This implies two things: a philosophical approach by way of ascent, leading to an understanding of the ultimate realities of the world and of being itself, by relating them to the God of revelation; and a theological approach by way of descent, bringing this same God down to the being of the world and its history. The material of this elucidation is the understanding of being, but of being as experienced by actual living according to Christ and the Church. This understanding is given by the Holy Spirit not to the isolated individual, but to the Church, in whose experience the individual has but a share, most of all the saint, who lets his own private experience be governed and molded entirely by that of the Church.

The explanation of man's being and history in the light of christology should be developed dogmatically in relation to the teaching of the Church about each of the persons of the Trinity. First, it must be developed into a doctrine about the creation, with reference to God the Father, creator of heaven and earth, a doctrine built on a christological foundation, on the relationship of Christ to the Father—in which we have been offered a participation after his death and resurrection. What the prayer of the saints, their experience of God in the world, might have to contribute to this doctrine has hardly begun to be explored.

But it is the Church's teaching on the second Person, christology, that stands to gain from what the saints experienced. In fact, however, christology also has remained practically static within the formal setting of Chalcedon; its further growth as a result of the total experience of the Church's faith is still awaited. We can see this if we consider the state of what might be called passiology (why have we no word for it?). The inner experiences of the Redeemer in his passion, which should constitute the center of the doctrine of redemption, are, admittedly, not to be understood by a comparison with purely human sufferings and states—unless we are to remain content with a purely external, legalistic doctrine of redemption. The sufferings of the Lord being, in virtue of the hypostatic union, *sui generis,* they were not just an intensification of common human sufferings. They were unique, since it was the only Son of the Father who suffered them; and so, in their essence, they have to be explained on trinitarian lines. The New Testament gives us very little that can serve to introduce us to the mysterious inner world of the passion. There is, however, more in the Old Testament, but it has never been made sufficient use of. Above all, there are the graces of participation in the passion given to the Church, the experiences of the saints, which are quite inexplicable except as a participation in Christ's states. These experiences constitute the vast, limitless field of the "dark nights," which, as described

73

by those who underwent them, are so strikingly similar and yet offer such a variety of individual aspects. To my knowledge, no theology has seriously undertaken the task of seeing them as a whole and evaluating them from the point of view of dogma (how else could it be done?). Not even writers on mysticism have assembled and subjected them to critical scrutiny. It may be objected that phenomena of this sort, when genuine, are unfitted for the common gaze; that the important thing about them is their effect, that it is of their nature to be hidden and inaccessible, for example in monasteries and convents. But this would be a strange notion of the catholicity of the redemption, as strange as to say that the fact that, on the Mount of Olives, the official representatives of the Church (including John) went to sleep, justifies, nay requires this neglect. Why should we persist in ignoring the detail of these sufferings, making not the least attempt to use, for a better understanding of the faith, these experiences so valuable for the Church? The important thing is not the "mystical phenomenon," nor even solely the co-redemptive function given as a grace, but the fact that something of the passion is, through the grace of the Head, constantly being made present in the body, and that the body needs to understand what is happening there by relating it to the Head as its source and end.

Something of the sort also holds good of the third article of the Church's teaching. The Holy Ghost is Christ present and acting in the heart of the Church and of each believer. The whole of ethics, all the holiness of the Church and the person, the whole of liturgy and contemplation find, in this article, their doctrinal setting, and need to be developed accordingly, in the light of all that the Church has experienced, which means, primarily, the experience of the saints. Much would appear in a very different light were we to apply our reflections to the archetypal function of the saints rather than to the figure presented by the average sinner, for example in the understanding of what a sacrament is and of what its reception means. What does it mean for a saint, when he communicates? He should know, and be able to teach us. What is the significance of a Christian life as a witness to Christ? What is its theoretical structure, and how is it realized in practice? The whole of apologetics also, as understood scripturally, comes within this third article. It was her Founder's will that the Church should prove herself to the world as the true Church through certain definite qualities. What are they, in the eyes of Christ, and what are they not? It is quite clear that the central point of Christ's apologetic, and equally of that of the apostles, is holiness. The Church commends herself to men through Christian love: "By this shall all men know." Whatever else we count as basic properties of the Church belongs to her structure, but has less appeal to the sincere inquirer. It is only when the Church is seen as the Church of saints that her image is irresistible. "If only all of you were like these . . ." is what the world says. Against the evidence of Christian love there is no valid objection, certainly not that derived from humanism, for Agape is essentially different from this.

These considerations are of general application, and not only to those outside the Church, for the Church can only be understood by her own members in her true nature, when viewed in the aspect of holiness. Holiness is the gift of purity made her by the bridegroom through the cleansing waters of the cross and baptism, a purity "without spot or wrinkle."

If the Church were not, in her essence, marial, were she not the bride, she could never be made comprehensible in all her hierarchical offices and functions. Logically, then, she would either have to abandon her authoritative claims (as in Protestantism) and content herself with merely drawing attention to the holiness of the Head: or else proceed to a complete divorce between authority and holiness, which would be still more incomprehensible. Admittedly the coincidence of these two spheres, as presented by Denis the Areopagite in the *Ecclesiastical Hierarchy,* remains an unattainable ideal; but it is only in view of this ideal that everything becomes meaningful and tolerable. It is, certainly, not enough to say that the hierarchical functions and the *opus operatum* are there on account of the inevitable sinfulness of the Church. This is true enough, but their presence does not mean the sanctioning of sin; it is the presence of the cross and the redemption. It is, therefore, only in function of the cross, and so of holiness, that the institutional side of the Church can be rightly interpreted.

4. BRIDE AND BRIDEGROOM

What all this amounts to is that theology in the Church proceeds always as a continuous dialogue between bridegroom and bride (of whom Mary is the prototype). The bridegroom gives and the bride receives; and only in this acceptance of faith can the miracle of the pouring forth of the Word, which is both sower and seed, be accomplished. In this respect, Bultmann and the form-historical method are perfectly right. With revelation there is no such thing as an objective, uncommitted, scientific "objectivity," but only a personal encounter of Word and faith, Christ and Church, in the mystery of the Canticle of Canticles. When she understands, then is the Church holy; and, insofar as she is holy, she understands. This law comprises both hierarchy and laity, each in its own mode. The hierarchy itself has its basis in the marial heart of the Church.

No one in recent years has had such a profound understanding of this law of theology, and applied it so thorougly, as M. J. Scheeben, for whom everything, even what is most formal, is related to the structure of the *Connubium.* At the center of his theology is the God-man with the two natures, whose union he interprets, with the Greek fathers, as the marriage of God with mankind in Mary's bridal chamber. The "personal" aspect is prominent in the relation of the Holy Spirit's overshadowing to the bridal act of faith of the virgin; the "physical" aspect, in her real motherhood and its fruit, the hypostatic union. For this reason, the patristic analogy for the latter, namely the relation of soul and body, in Aristotelian terms that of form and matter, is interpreted from the standpoint of the *Connubium,* which gives the whole Thomistic philosophy a theological aspect, or, in Scheeben's words, transforms it in the light of theology. The whole structure of the world is, also, seen to derive from a relation of love, a nuptial relation. Scheeben consistently applies his basic theme all through theology. He makes it the foundation of the formal relationships of the natural and the supernatural, of reason and faith, and also of the process of justification, of the nature and workings of actual and habitual grace, and, naturally, of the theology of the life of Christ, of the relations between Christ and the Church, of the Eucharist and all the sacraments, even of scripture and inspiration. Everything is, for him, a revelation of the love of the Trinity, the *theios eros*.

Consequently it is not surprising that Scheeben, both in *The Mysteries of Christianity* and in his dogmatic theology, puts the greatest emphasis on the action of the Holy Spirit in purifying and enlightening, where the work of the theologian is concerned. He quotes Paul in this connection: *Animalis homo non percipit quae sunt Spiritus Dei.* He considers the moral disposition, purity of heart and humility, to be still more important. "The Holy Spirit anoints with his light the spiritual eye, and so imparts a moral receptivity enabling us to attain a fuller and purer comprehension of the content of faith; and so our knowledge only comes to full strength and life through the *realizing* of the supernatural life flowing out within us from the Spirit." This alone is what places us "in the most inward communication" with the realities of faith, "sets before our inward eye a living image of them, makes us taste and feel them, and endows them with an affinity and intimacy with us." The action of the Holy Spirit in theology sets the final seal on the character of supernatural holiness that befits it in virtue of its source, its object and its end, which is why the older theologians called theology, in an absolute sense, "*doctrina sacra.*" Scheeben also considered this character of holiness to be communicated to it by the Church, since she watches over the course theology takes much more closely than over other disciplines. Theology, therefore, participates in a special manner in the bridal holiness of the Church.

Theology, as dialogue between bride and bridegroom in the unity and communication of the Spirit, continually brings to light new modes of union and interpenetration.

It is, in the first place, contemplation of the bridegroom by the bride, and this becomes more objective, profound and comprehensive, the more light and grace are imparted by the bridegroom to the bride. In his light she sees his light, and therein "beholding the glory of the Lord with open face, is transformed into the same image from glory to glory, as by the Spirit of the Lord" (2 Cor 3:18). The purpose of contemplation is to cause the life of the bride to be transformed: glory is the splendor of holiness, which is not only mirrored in the bride, but takes her up into the "metamorphosis." This does not mean that the bride should set about contemplating in herself the glory of the bridegroom, but that what he imparts to her is of the same nature as himself, something of the christological order. To this belong all higher graces of vision and knowledge. They are participations in the Son's own vision and knowing, and range from the gifts of the Holy Spirit to the strictly mystical charismata and experiences of God. Here, too, belong the graces manifest in the life of saints, which, according to Paul, are themselves charismata, and so functions of the mystical body, functions we have already seen to be not without profound theological significance. For the saints are not given to us to admire for their heroic powers, but that we should be enlightened by them on the inner reality of Christ, both for our better understanding of the faith and for our living thereby in charity. As Martin Buber says: "The lives of such men need a theological commentary; their own words are a contribution to this, but a very fragmentary one," and its completion is reserved to us. The life of the saints is theology in practice. Whether they have said, or could have said, much or little in the way of interpretation hardly matters; but the beholder, when it is a matter of specified missions, must always presuppose that there is more to be seen than an example, however striking, of something already known.

The example of Garrigou-Lagrange might well be followed in his confronting the theology of Thomas with the mystical experience of John of the Cross, carefully assessing both from a theological standpoint, making them elucidate and complete each other. Whether or not we agree with all his conclusions, his initiative and method are certainly to be commended. Though objective revelation was concluded with the death of the last apostle, it does not follow that, in the Church of saints, nothing further happens that touches on revelation. After all, the miracles of absolution and the consecration are continually repeated, and they bring about, again and again, a new presence of the events of Good Friday and Easter within the Church. Why should it not be the same with the constant repetition of the theological existence of the Lord in the life of his faithful and saints?

The life common to Christ and the Church is the context of a living and realized theology, in the sense of actual life poised between perdition and redemption, sinfulness and sanctity. The existence of sin within the field of force of grace, the impact, here and now, between despairing obduracy and crucified love, these, and not a colorless and static world of philosophy, are the matter of theology. This is why it cannot be expressed *solely* in the sleek and passionless form of the treatise, but demands movement, sharp debate (*quaestio disputata*), the virile language of deep and powerful emotion—the sort of language used by Augustine, Richard or Gerhoh, Bonaventure, Pascal or Kierkegaard—

80

a dialectic pushed to the limit in order to rouse and inflame.

Theology speaks of an event so unique, so extraordinary that it is never permissible to abstract from it—as Husserl does, for instance, methodically bracketing [*ausklammert*] all that is factual. There is always a tendency in human thought—and theology is no exception—to bracket the concrete and forget it. We are prone to look on historical revelation as a past event, as presupposed, and not as something always happening, to be listened to and obeyed; and it is this that becomes the matter of theological reflection.

The saints have always been on guard against such an attitude, and immersed themselves in the actual circumstances of the events of revelation. They desired to be present, when and where each thing happened. With Mary they sit at the feet of Jesus, hearing from his own mouth the words of revelation. They want to know what the Lord says to them, and nothing else. They do not want to stop listening, not for a single moment, to what is being revealed, as though the content of revelation were an event long since concluded, over and done with, something there to be examined and probed like any other object of science. Their dealings are with God and him exclusively. Everything, even what they know already, they wish to hear from him, as if they had never heard it before. They wish to have the world explained anew, interpreted afresh, in the light of revelation. They wish to contemplate nature with no other eyes than those of Christ. They have no desire to know God as simply *ens a se,* but solely as the Father of Christ; the Spirit, too, not as an abstract world of universal laws and prescriptions, but as the Spirit of the tongues of fire, the Spirit who breathes where he wills. They are almost fanatically ex-

81

clusivists, for they see this approach as the surest way to the universality and catholicity of the truth. They are not perturbed about how to reconcile the supernatural and the natural orders, faith and reason, the secular and the ecclesiastical spheres, for they know that those whose standpoint is firmly fixed in Christ are relieved of concern for these, though not of the practical duties that follow, of concern, that is, for the unity in question, but not of the mission to the world that this unity involves. The discharge of their Christian vocation, even if it be that of thinker and theologian, does not require them to abandon their standpoint in Christ. Christ himself is God's emissary to the world, and he, likewise, sends them, with the promise to be with them all days, even to the end of the world. Even in accommodating themselves to the various languages of the world, they do not do so smoothly, like diplomats, but on the strength of the pentecostal miracle, which enables the unchanging miracle to be conveyed in any system of thought or conceptual idiom.

In saying that their constant aim is to steep themselves in the stream of life ever issuing from the mouth of the eternal Word, we have tacitly indicated the form of theology. Their one desire is to be receptive, men of prayer in other words. Their theology is essentially an act of adoration and prayer. This is the tacit presupposition of any systematic theology, the air that courses through the systems, the thought-form out of which it is born and in which it develops. Christian dogmatics must express the fact that one whose thinking is dictated by faith is in a constant relationship of prayer with its object. One has only to read Anselm: "I cannot seek you, if you do not teach me how, nor find if you do not show yourself." In prayer he draws closer to the mystery; in prayer he embarks on his most abstract reasoning on God and his attributes; prayer guides him as he embodies his experiment in thought, as he momentarily and methodically sets aside and breaks off the act of faith, in order to release the whole force of the *rationes necessariae*. In prayer he receives the supernatural revelation of God in Christ, and so comes to see that God's natural revelation in creation and man's reason is also revelation in the true sense, and that it must be approached in the same spirit as the historical revelation itself—on one's knees. Anselm does not distinguish between the natural and the supernatural, knowledge and faith, as between the profane and the sacred; for he learned by faith that reason too was created for the sake of faith, nature for the sake of grace, and that both form, by their interconnection, a single revelation of the incomprehensible love of the Trinity. Prayer is the *realistic* attitude in which the mystery must be approached: obedient faith, the "presuppositionless," is the attitude where theology is concerned, because it corresponds to the *tabula rasa* of love, in which the heart awaits all and anticipates nothing. This attitude, which is that of prayer, is never superseded or outdistanced by the attitude demanded by knowledge.

Knowledge must never be separated from the attitude of prayer with which it began. It can no more do so than gnosis could outstrip faith, and indeed it is an inner form of faith: "faith that seeks understanding." "Seeking" here is a radical, indwelling property of faith which, deprived of it, would cease to be faith. Even when found, God is still he who is sought (*"ut inventus quaeratur, immensus est"*: Augustine, *In Joan. tr.* 63, 1), and faith fulfilled is still

83

praying, asking, adoring faith. There is no such thing as a theological investigation that does not breathe the atmosphere of "seeking in prayer." It is the sign by which the saint comes to know whether this or that form of the truth concerns him, and when to find the air in which he can breathe and flourish. Prayerful theology does not mean "affective theology" as opposed to theology properly so called, and strictly scientific. The antithesis is merely superficial, and invalidated by the exact, and very often abstract studies of Anselm and Albert, not to mention Thomas. Theology must always be conducted with rigorous precision. But it must also correspond at all points with its object, itself unique among objects of knowledge; and conform to its special content and method. This means that, judged by the standard of the purely natural sciences, the methodologies most comfortable to their object will have a kind of amateurish flavor. Augustine hardly spoke dispassionately in the Confessions and in the Enarrationes; but he was no less a theologian. Or did scientific theology only begin with Peter Lombard? Yet none dealt more adequately with matters of theology than Cyril of Jerusalem, Origen in his homilies, Gregory of Nazianzen and the Areopagite, the master whose works are so full of the spirit of awe and wonder. Who would be so bold as to say of any of the fathers that his works are "full of unction" in the modern sense? In those days, men were quite clear as to how theology should be written: it should reflect both the unity of faith and knowledge and an attitude of objectivity allied with one of reverence and awe. Theology was, when pursued by men of sanctity, a theology at prayer; which is why its fruitfulness for prayer, its power to foster prayer, is so undeniable.

As time went on, theology at prayer was superseded by theology at the desk, and this brought about the cleavage now under discussion. "Scientific" theology became more and more divorced from prayer, and so lost the accent and tone with which one should speak of what is holy, while "affective" theology, as it became increasingly empty, often degenerated into unctious, platitudinous piety. It was in this way responsible for the parallel decline in Christian art, which threatens to disintegrate into a "modern" realism devoid of awe and reverence, and on the other hand into a romanticism remote from reality.

There is no question of turning back the wheel of history, and proposing a renascence of patristic theology at the expense of scholasticism. The progress wrought by scholasticism is obvious. Even so, it is of the very essence of tradition, and so of theology, that its progress depends on a deeper, bolder exploration of the sources, not only of the very young sources of scripture, whose theological exploration is always in its initial stages, as we feel now more than ever, but of the living spring of patristic theology, whose imposing structure and inexhaustible riches are surely a gift of providence to succeeding generations. There are any number of theses deserving of development which the fathers initiated, and which, subsequently, as theology became systematized, were held unsuitable, unimportant, and so left in abeyance, a process of exclusion carried further, and with rapidity, in scholasticism from the late middle ages to the present. What a wealth of material is to be found in Thomas, what a variety of approaches and aspects he suggests, how numerous the hints and promptings scattered at random through his works, compared with the dry bones of a modern textbook! It is true these were written for learners, but, after all, the great scholastics had pupils, even beginners in view, and had to make everything as clear, simple and incontrovertible as possible. In any case, must Catholic theology always remain at the textbook level? Surely it may look sometimes beyond the *haplousteroi,* the vulgar (which, in the sense of the fathers, are not the uneducated, but those content with a cursory acquaintance with the faith), and enter on the depths of divine revelation, speaking, under Paul's guidance, "wisdom among the perfect," "the wisdom of God in a mystery, a wisdom which is hidden, which God ordained before the world, unto our glory" (1 Cor 2:6–7).

SPIRITUALITY

It is of the essence of God's word to be sown and developed in the field which is the heart of man, and only in the fleeting instant of its acceptance is it grasped as an objective entity; or rather, on further reflection, even this is impossible, since the act of faith in the divine word is itself an indispensable condition for it to be perceived in its objective reality. There is no neutral standpoint outside the encounter between bride and bridegroom, no objective standpoint, that is, from which it is possible to survey and assess the mystery of the revelation in which both are involved (the bridegroom as freely imparting it, the bride as responding). The only question, then, is: who responds, whose act of faith prepares the development of an understanding of revelation, a dogmatic theology in the widest sense. The answer must be conditioned from the outset by the fact that the bride is, primarily, the Church, the mother of all believers and prior to them, not the resultant of a number of individuals taken together. This is true of the Church even though she is visibly manifest only in her members, were they no more than "two or three" gathered together in the name of the Lord.

Accordingly if spirituality is the subjective aspect of

dogmatic theology, the word of God as received by the
bride and developing within her, then spirituality must
necessarily exhibit an analogous form: that is, it must be
an absolute unity, inasmuch as the subject is the Church
herself, the individual being a subject only by participation
in the Church; and it must also be manifold inasmuch as the
Church is actually existing, is always a *universale in rebus,*
that is, *in personis.* The unity of this analogy only becomes
apparent to the spiritual doctrine of the fathers and the
middle ages in the marial mystery, for Mary as bride constitutes a third element, mediating between the *virgo ecclesia*
and the *virgo anima:* as that of an individual, on the plane of
the *anima,* and yet, through her privileged place in the
economy of salvation, she is the "subjective model" and the
ground of the fruitfulness of the Church as an a priori
reality, insofar as the Church is distinct from her Founder,
Christ, with a life of her own. Thus, the unity of the bride
is not an abstract idea, but is the unity of an individual
subject; and so it is clear that "marial spirituality" is not on
a plane with other spiritualities in the Church. For if it is
truly marial, and not just a special devotion to Mary according to individual inclination, this spirituality is what makes
the objective teaching of the Church come alive in the
individual, and, at the same time, it frees the individual
from his limitations by making him realize in practice the
full wealth of the Church's teaching. This is what is involved
in the character of the Church as bride, as taught in her
tradition, explicitly from the time of Origen's commentary
on the Canticle, and systematized in the medieval commentators, for instance William of St. Thierry. The aware-
ness of this is what prevented the whole question of Chris-

tian spirituality from being confined to the fruitless enquiry as to whether it is one or many. Every individual spirituality is, while not ceasing to be individual, at the same time, in a real sense, the whole of spirituality (of course, only in the bridal function, that of responding to revelation, not in the creative function of the bridegroom). Consequently each particular element has a qualified participation in the whole. It is not only a part, as a limb is part of the body with a specialized function (Paul's image falls short at this point), but is also a special form of the totality, as, for instance, each monad (if such there be) mirrors in itself the totality of all monads, indeed is an integrating and integrated stage of the totality itself.

This brings out the full meaning of spirituality. *On the one hand*, there exists a uniform *theologia spiritualis,* consisting in the Church's objective teaching on how revelation is to be realized in practice, in the life of faith, hope and charity. And since such a life has its own laws and degrees, it follows that at least its basic features and structures form part of dogmatic theology. It is the Holy Spirit who, poured forth into our hearts, impresses on them the truth of the Son; and, therefore, this *theologia spiritualis* comes under the article: *"Credo in Spiritum Sanctum . . . vivificantem."* It is the same Spirit who conducts the believer from the exterior, catechism stage to an inner understanding of the "deep things of God," to the "wisdom of God in a mystery" (1 Cor 2:7); and so this same theology is simply the Church's dogmatic theology at its profoundest level, that of mystery. It is what was known as *theologia mystica* by the fathers and even by the medievals up to the twelfth century. It was only when the Spanish writers put much greater emphasis on the subjective experiencing of the mysteries that the word "*mysticus*" came to take on its modern meaning, and then, in order to comprise the whole of man's subjective relationship to Christian truth, it had to be supplemented by the idea of "*askesis*." Consequently *theologia spiritualis,* by a rather doubtful process of simplification, came to be known, particularly in the nineteenth century, as ascetical-mystical theology, in which asceticism denoted the active work of the individual, and mysticism his increasingly passive experience of divine things. As a result of this pragmatic, psychological approach, the content of revelation was transposed into a subjective framework, and so the idea of the Word as bridegroom, always present in the old *theologia spiritualis* or *mystica,* was almost completely lost. This produced a fatal cleavage between a "dogmatic theology" divorced from the subject and turned in on itself, and the psychological subject standing opposed to it; and, since there was no center in which they could meet, the separation persisted.

The theology of the fathers, and that of the middle ages, was *doctrina sacra,* both in its object and in its form: it retained both the spiritual dimension of the objective mystery and of the Holy Spirit's initiation not merely in general as a vague atmosphere ("unction"), but at every stage of thought, in the work, for instance, of Augustine, Anselm, William of Auvergne, and Bonaventure. Chenu and Hayen have attempted to bring out the fact that this is also, fundamentally, the case with Thomas, though his main object was to apply all the techniques of reasoning to establish theology, in the face of the exact sciences then emerging, as itself a science, and not only a spiritual "wisdom." But those

90

who could no longer discern the spiritual medium always present in Thomas as the atmosphere presupposed by his work, and who were, moreover, infected by the modern scientific attitude, used all their endeavors to make theology conform to the ideals of modern science, and so were bound to bring about the cleavage already alluded to: dogmatic theology on the one hand, on the other a spirituality of the empirical subject; and this confirmed the parallel process of *theologia moralis* emancipating itself from dogmatic theology. The problem, we must be quite clear, by no means consists in the inevitable and progressive relative independence of the various disciplines with the advance of theological study; if this were the case, the synthetic standpoint could be easily regained at any moment. What impedes the reintegration of dogmatic and spiritual theology so disastrously is the loss of the objective spiritual medium of which the old theology was so conscious as it proceeded in its development. Certainly the fathers had at their disposal all the rational methods of distinguishing and defining for the clarification of concepts; they were used in the fierce controversies with heretics, both by individual theologians and by councils. But the crucial point is that these methods were not the determining factor in the construction of their theology. Even polemical works such as Irenaeus' *Adversus Haereses,* Athanasius' *Contra Arianos,* Hilary's *De Trinitate,* Gregory of Nyssa's *Contra Eunomium* were embedded in a spiritual, sapiential setting which became more and more pronounced as the decisive element.

It may well be harder in our day, when we have come to set so much store by logical procedure, to bring out this spiritual dimension clearly enough in theology. Yet it is of

91

the utmost importance to see that what is lacking is not just
a piece of material that can be easily incorporated into the
existing structure, or else a sort of stylistic quality to be reproduced anew (though, occasionally, modern mystical and
sapiential theology may be taken for the real thing, as Neo-
gothic for genuine Gothic). The fact is that the spiritual
dimension can only be recovered through the soul of man
being profoundly moved as a result of his direct encounter
with revealed truth, so that it is borne in upon him, once
and for all, how the theologian should think and speak, and
how he should not. This holds good for both the estranged
disciplines, dogmatic theology and spirituality. Here, however, we are concerned with the latter; and so we would
point out that the spirituality of the *grand siècle,* that of
Ignatius, Teresa, John of the Cross, Pascal, Francis de Sales,
Lallemant, Balthasar Alvarez, Berulle and Condren, Fénelon and Madame Guyon, Marie de l'Incarnation and
Caussade, despite their proclivity to empirical and psychological considerations, was essentially orientated (as were
the medievals from Bernard to Henry Suso) to the theological act, with all it involves, in which the "bride" responds
to the call and self-giving of the "bridegroom." This is the
source whence the spirituality of the time drew its quality of
implacable gravity (beneath all the baroque adornment),
the remorseless exigence of the *Más* and *Indiferencia* of
Ignatius, of the *Nada* of John of the Cross, the *Amour Pur*
of Fénelon, the *Abandon* of Caussade, of Bérulle's doctrine
of the mirrowing of Christ's *états* in the life of the soul, of
Condren's theory of sacrifice that verges on a theological
nihilism; even of Francis de Sales (and plainer still in
Jeanne de Chantal) who, under all the exuberant imagery of

92

the *"Theotimus,"* teaches how real love is stripped and purified by all kinds of pains, derelictions and hells. The main object in view with all of them was to lay open the pure, naked structure of the bridal response, and so of a crucial element of dogmatic and—whether explicitly or implicitly—of marial theology. It is the task of a future history of theology in its totality to survey and assess this whole field.

On the other side, we have a multiplicity of "spiritualities" in contrast with the uniform dogmatic and authoritative *theologia spiritualis;* and it is only at this point that those shades of difference emerge which move the present time either to enthusiasm or disquiet. The very multiplicity of historic personalities points to qualitative differences between them, and still more to God's revelation being adapted to their special characters. The existence of such differences was not, of course, strange to tradition, since it is so very clearly rooted in revelation itself, insofar as it took the form of a history gradually unfolding through the ages in a series of new encounters of the divine Spirit with different peoples, and in all kinds of religious, cultural and political situations. The "spirituality" of the desert is different from that of the promised land; that of the judges different from that of the kings, that of the prophets different again, and especially that of the sapiential books. The Old Testament itself makes it plain enough that it is not solely a matter of different standpoints from which men view an identical object; though this should not be ignored: the light of revelation grew in proportion to the growth of the

93

people's minds and of their receptivity to what was always present there since Yahweh began to go with Israel. Besides this change of standpoint, there was also a change in the content of what was revealed, corresponding to the changed situation, but this, in its turn, was something brought about by God and a mode of revelation. This, in fact, explains why it was that the people so often refused to conform. It is never possible to infer, as regards the biblical narrative, a future situation, in its bearing on revelation, from a present one, even when the believer is given an assurance that his faith will persist and respond to God's word, whatever surprises it may bring. The same process of change is even more pronounced in the New Testament, since there the long period of waiting, the time of the promise, condenses into a single moment, that of fulfillment. Christ, in every encounter with an individual to whom a mission of a special kind is given, introduces some element peculiar to each case. Peter and John, Paul and James, Martha and Mary, the Magdalen, Lazarus, the Samaritan woman: these are all unique cases of encounter of Christ with the individual; yet, in each, the whole, indivisible Christ communicates himself.

No small part of what the word is intended to convey comes from comparing and contrasting different aspects and standpoints. It is not merely that we gain thereby a general sense of an infinity of perspectives, but precise notions of the nature of the Church, for example, of life in the Christian community, of the irreducibility of Christian ways of life; *spiritualia spiritualibus comparantes,* we come to sense new *spiritualia.* For this reason, tradition has never taken a stand against variations as such, provided they are

94

kept within the unity of the Church. Divergences occasioned, at times, a certain acrimony; how they could be compatible within Catholic unity was often not at first apparent, and only after some friction between their protagonists could the way be opened. Of this process, the disputes between the apostles, arising from their differing missionary standpoints, as recorded in the Acts, are in some way a prototype. Origen repeatedly observed that there must necessarily be, within the Church, a variety of schools and standpoints for the fullness of the one Logos to be brought out and expressed in human language. The fathers, with their vigorous, perhaps even intransigent sense of the unity of the Church (anyone departing from it they considered lost), had an equally strong feeling for the individuality of the great doctors (see Jerome, *De viris illustribus*). In fact, the East had it in greater measure than the West, and, despite the preeminent contribution of Augustine, remained the inexhaustibly fecund source of spiritual theology. Its products range from the unsystematized and varied "experiences" and diversified practices of the desert fathers to the starkly intellectual mystical doctrine of Evagrius; the subtle teachings about inner experience of Diadochus of Photica and the homilies of Macarius; the severe, pure evangelism of Basil; and the wholly new contribution of the Areopagite writings.

The vast range of possibilities latent in the word, giving rise continually to fresh ones in the course of development, is shown by the almost infinite variety of distinct specialities appearing in the twelfth century (recently summarized by Chenu and Leclerq). It followed on a period of timid traditionalism, the early middle ages, which in its devotion to

95

unity in the abstract discouraged all diversity. At the same time, the question of the different states of persons in the Church was first raised in acute form; the monastic state, the regular and secular clergy, the laity became conscious of their qualitative differences, and disputes arose from each taking a standpoint appropriate to their ecclesiastical status. It was only when Francis and Dominic took their place beside Benedict that there came into full view the mysterious force of founder-personalities, a force dimly perceived as issuing from the very core of revelation. This force was due to a special quality bestowed on them and inseparable from their personalities as supernaturally molded; it enabled them to impart a special stamp, something far deeper than a mere psychological imprint, on a spiritual "family," and so, perhaps for the first time, to exhibit what we now call a "special spirituality." It is a gift of the highest order, but it entails a grave risk, that of misinterpreting the charisma of the founder, and of focusing the mind on the image presented by the saint, instead of on Christ. This happened with the Franciscan spirituals, and the menace is always present to those who are not sufficiently on their guard. Ignatius, with his rules for thinking with the Church, warned his followers against opposing saint to saint and one way to another. The basic reason why there are different spiritualities is not because revealed truth is expressed in human terms; nor are they due primarily to historical conditions, or to the elements superimposed on the objective doctrine by its embodiment in the experience of different individuals. All these factors have their validity in a theological view, but they are subordinate to the *free* distribution, by the Head of the Church, of his gifts and charismata (1 Cor

12:4–11: Eph 4:11–13: *Unicuique datur manifestatio Spiritus ad utilitatem—dividens singulis prout vult—ipse dedit quosdam apostolos*). Consequently the chief ground of the special characteristics of a spirituality is not the person who propounds it, but the mission from above, which cannot be adjudged and confined in empirical, psychological terms. For since it springs from a transcendental source, the free disposition of the Head, its end and mode of action must also be transcendent, and therefore what it contributes to the fullness of the mystical body is incapable of precise assessment. The real significance of any particular mode of spirituality is in the fact that its source and authentication is in heaven. It exists not for its own sake, but for Christ and the Church, and this implies a further element, the marial, which we shall now proceed to consider.

A spirituality centered on the attitude exemplified by Mary is, we have already seen, not just one spirituality among others. For this reason, although Mary is an individual believer and, as such, the prototype and model of all response in faith, she resolves all particular spiritualities into the one spirituality of the bride of Christ, the Church. What we learn from Mary, a lesson valid for all times, is that the response of the handmaid of the Lord to the Word working in her all his will—in such a special and unique manner—is not just one particular theme in theology. What is special in Mary's spirituality is the radical renunciation of any special spirituality other than the overshadowing of the Most High and the indwelling of the divine Word. Humanly speaking, her cooperation with God consists only

97

in the service every mother renders to her child, inspired not by reflection on the nature of "motherhead," but simply by her perception of the child's needs. Only thus could Mary's response be made, through grace, so complete and perfect as to become the perfect response of the bride, the Church, and the form of all the responses made by individual believers. The idea of making marial spirituality one among others is, therefore, a distortion, as dangerous as attempting to claim for one's own particular way the status of "the spirituality of the Church." This may be obscured by the concept of hyperdulia, which on a superficial level can lead to an emphasis on Mary's special status through the glorification of her personal privileges; but the real point of the "hyper" is that it transcends all that is particular in spirituality, merging devotion to Mary in the general one of loving veneration for the *Virgo-mater Ecclesia,* which as body, bride and fullness of Christ is herself a part of our faith (*credo Ecclesiam catholicam*).

There is one conclusion to be drawn from this for all missions and vocations that come within the general field of marial spirituality. It applies whether these are relatively special, in the sense of pertaining to an ecclesiastical state or office or a religious order, or of all absolutely personal vocations or individual charismata. These special spiritualities are only so in the marial and ecclesiastical sense, if they avoid all preoccupation with their particular characteristics and look, with the eyes of Mary, on the unique object, so as to find in him, from *his* law and requirements, the rule for their own conduct and response. After all, we can hardly imagine Francis, for instance, preoccupied with "Franciscanism" instead of with the poverty of Christ, in the light of which

98

all the graces and gifts of the Holy Spirit were imparted to him. The great founders were, generally, unwilling to formulate in set terms the nature of the work entrusted to them; and when they did so, they observed the laws of natural and supernatural prudence, always aware of the limited influence of a single life even in the Church; nor did they attribute the place accorded them in the Church to a "spirituality" regarded as something in its own right, with its own claim to greatness. For them, their mission, office or function was not *id quod,* but a *medium in quo,* a species *im-* or *expressa,* which, quite unself-consciously, led to an understanding of reality. To continue the analogy, we might say that the more perfect the species, the deeper and more comprehensive the understanding of the real object. For this reason, it is precisely the "great missions," those most distinctive and striking, that most faithfully embody and reflect the very core and content of the "thing itself," the gospel of Christ, so that, between them, there subsists a real community of being (*circumincessio*), without confusion (*asynchytos*). What we find in the worldly sphere is equally true of the Church: while the "great" among the spirituals and mystics agree with one another (without recourse to "syncretism"), the "schools" attached to them disagree and quarrel. This happens because the former keep their gaze firmly and freely on the thing itself, while their followers make their "master" their primary concern, and, next to this, the mode in which he viewed the world and modeled it; and, only in the third place, the world itself thus formed. The one certain thing about Goethe is that he was no "Goethean," about Thomas that he was no Thomist. Great men communicate with one another not in their

99

forms, but in the depth of the reality made known to them through these forms. The special and peculiar nature of their form does not cut them off from one another; it is, in fact, their medium of communication.

Undoubtedly some missions have a more strongly individual stamp than others, and so too have the spiritualities that correspond to them. For example, the tasks belonging to a particular state of life (the priesthood, the married state, the religious state) are, as such, far more general than the special tasks, say, of a founder; and some charismata are more general, some more particular. But although the bride's answer is the general form of spirituality, it is not general in the sense of being generic, but is something highly particular and definite. So that we cannot say that the less pronouncedly individual charismata and tasks are at a disadvantage over against the others, since, as we have seen, the more distinctive ones only possess the quality in order to transcend it more strikingly in pointing to the general. The anonymous character shared by the less distinctive tasks is that of the bride herself; it is Mary's desire to avoid all prominence in the presence of the divine Word alone occupying the foreground. One thing is very plain: anyone who tries to compensate an institution or way of life for any lack of special charismatic distinctiveness in its origins, by reflecting on its spirituality, and not only formulating but exaggerating it, stylizing it, making good the lacunae and, when necessary, embroidering a bit here and there—much as one invents a foundation-myth—is not only guilty of a piece of appalling theological bad taste, productive of narrow-mindedness, sterility and the horrors of "sanctuary art," but sins against the essential structure of the Church, and diffuses an atmosphere of sectarianism and heresy. Unfortunately this is not merely a theoretical consideration. Quite apart from certain calamitous instances, there has been a fairly widespread outbreak of "special" spiritualities. Every little association (the more exclusive, the better) tries to incubate its own particular "spirit," around which it knocks up some kind of structure, as if engaged in creating a work of art. Love's labor lost! Unless the Lord build the house, they that build it labor in vain. In the introduction to my book on Teresa of Lisieux, I observed, in regard to the undue pressing of claims for canonization, that it is God who makes saints and presents them to the Church for canonization; and, though we cannot say that he has left no scope for the free exercise of the Church's judgment, yet the Church's liberty is essentially bound up with obedience to the bridegroom, with looking and listening to him. Time and effort spent in pushing the merits of a particular spirituality are stolen from the service of the one thing necessary; and it is not difficult to see that the particular form becomes, unconsciously, the central concern, while the thing itself is relegated to the status of a means serving *ad majorem gloriam* of the order, the congregation, or some other group or movement.

It will not be surprising if we extend this warning to the so-called spirituality of the ecclesiastical states. Although there is a sense in which we can speak of a spirituality of the counsels, of the married state, of the priestly state, it is in practice impossible to contrast these forms of spirituality as distinct and precisely demarcated. After all, they are not like works of art whose laws we can master, or like new clothes we can try on so as to live a Christian life in style. That sort of thing is estheticism, and quite out of place, incompatible with the real beauty of the Christian life. This trend of thinking, even when found in certain sections of a great religious order, is an infallible sign of decadence. It is, however, true to say that there seem to be moments in the history of the Church when a particular state of life becomes more conscious of its special task and function than before, and, through reflection, frees itself from its previous dormancy. We can see this, for example, in the history of the secular clergy, particularly of parish priests, while today seems to be the time of the laity, which, having attained its majority, needs an appropriate spirituality, and one no longer governed by the standards and categories of the religious state. But much of what has been done in this line is quite superficial and trite, since the ecclesiastical states are treated as though they were separate departments of a secular association, without due attention to the profound mysteries of the ontology of the Church and the resultant circumincession of the various states. As a result, many of these attempts savor of the fruitless activism so characteristic of our time (*sicut foenum arescit*), instead of being the outcome of a genuine mission of the Holy Spirit.

One certain means for the discernment of spirits is to test the presence, open or latent, of a certain ill-feeling toward other states of life or forms of spirituality. There is no doubt that the ecclesiastical atmosphere in Europe and America is troubled by some such sentiment on the part of the laity toward the hierarchy, of the laity and the secular clergy jointly toward the religious orders, and, at the same time, of the orders and the clergy together against an "emancipated laity." Antipathies of this kind within the Church cannot serve to build up the body of Christ (Eph 4:12), nor does any good come of discrediting the religious state, on the ground that it was instituted by the Church in the course of history, and can well be dispensed with. Yet, precisely because the Church's structure is given from above, something mysterious and not a merely human contrivance, it can, while retaining its basic form (the hierarchy and the forms of life derived from the sacraments), be susceptible of modifications, the outcome of a living dialogue between the various states, one in which the whole Church is concerned. In this way, new forms may make their appearance, which, though rooted in tradition and in the supratemporal nature of the Church, have a fresh, distinctive stamp, and are truly the work of the Holy Spirit. Among these we may include foundations like the Little Brothers and Sisters of Père de Foucauld, certain secular institutes and movements such as that of Abbé Pierre. We can only hope that these, and others like them, will resist the temptation to assign themselves their own form of spirituality to be consciously cultivated, instead of desiring nothing more than a humble following of Christ in self-abnegation. Today Christianity can only bring influence to bear through what is poor, interior, hidden, simple and genuine; and this alone is enough to show how repellent and profound must be the effect produced by the purveyors of specially cultivated spiritualities.

This will suffice in the way of criticism. It should serve to establish the positive factor, which is the mystery of the marial disposition, as comprising and summing up the whole responsiveness of the bride to the bridegroom, under the prompting of the Spirit. What is of the highest significance here is that Mary, in her office, could, being "full of grace," combine in perfect harmony states of life otherwise incompatible: virginity and motherhood, the married and the religious state, even in a real, though analogous or eminent mode, the priesthood (as coredemptrix) and the lay state. She represents the higher unity, not indeed as a superhuman being, but on our own human and Christian level. Thereby she shows conclusively how deeply involved with one another are the various states, and how irrelevant it is to set them in opposition by viewing them from a far lower level, where their incompatibility is most in evidence.

The circumincession in Mary of the different states of life and of what they involve is, of course, a participation in Christ's own transcendence of them, as God and man. But he transcends them as their creative source, possessing each of them *eminenter,* the priesthood, the religious, the married state (in the eucharistic and redemptive mystery of the one flesh). It is in this latter regard that Christ's celibacy represents in visible form the immutable order and hierarchy of the states of life, and to deny this hierarchical order (as does the modern theology of marriage, whether openly or by implication) is again a sign of a rebellious spirit. Nothing good can come of proscribing a theological tradition of the ancient Church, worked out over more than a thousand years, concerning the state of man in paradise, in the name of the "claims" of modern marriage theology. Louis Bouyer, whom no one can tax with narrowness of view, upholds against it the nobler conception, showing that Augustine's position is not simply to be discarded as though it were due to latent Manichaeism, since even "the Greek fathers, the most independent of Augustinian influence, have also, in their fashion, opinions quite the reverse of the idyllic conceptions of sexuality current among Catholics at the present time. . . . This solution, so reasonable and reassuring, is liable to foster certain illusions, as we see only too well nowadays."[1] Even if the position of Thomas has prevailed as the accepted theology of marriage (in this, Müller's view is correct), nevertheless the mystery is far deeper than a superficial theology of the states of life might lead us to suppose. The circumincession of the states and of their spiritualities in Jesus and Mary point back to a mystery in the original paradisal state, whose archetypal but impenetrable[2] nature forbids us to deduce from it, by an arbitrary selection of isolated factors, complete spiritualities of the various states.

We must not, however, stop short with Christ. He is, indeed, wholly the Word of God and the revelation of the triune divine life, that is, of the circumincession of the three Persons in a single nature, and so of three divine "states" and "spiritualities." The coming of the Person of the Son in Jesus Christ and the visible manifestation of his relationships to the Father and the Spirit forbid us to resign ourselves, in a spirit of agnosticism, to the view that all distinction, being caught up in the identity of the divine essence, eludes us. The divine unity is one of fullness and not of a bare abstraction; we approach it (here Nicholas of Cusa and Hegel were right) by thinking together all that exists separately in the world, and so begin to be aware of the meaning and the possibility of distinctions. If, as we have

[1] *Woman and Man with God,* London, 56, 58.
[2] As though a few scraps of philosophy were all we need to be cognizant of the dialectic of this primordial state, a dialectic impenetrable to the understanding (of *natura lapsa,* even though *reparata*) which the fathers approached with such reverence.

shown, spiritualities in the Church have their source from above, in the qualitative richness of the world of grace, then the ultimate basis both of their unity and distinction must be in the Trinity. Here is the original and native place of the "identity of identity and nonidentity," and it is the only point from which to interpret their reflection in the communication of missions within the mystical body. This reflection signifies that a "relative opposition" of personal standpoints is permitted and required, and these are irreducible to one another only insofar as they are absolutely "relative" to one another and (by reason of their origin) apart. Any other explanation of the divine Persons than a relational one would be inconsistent with the divine life of love. A mission, and therefore a spirituality, in the Church may be predominantly marked by the characteristics of the Father, the Son or the Spirit, but this fact must at once present itself in the form of a participation by grace in the mysteries of the personal relationships, of generation and spiration, both active and passive. Certainly we cannot construct an adequate trinitarian typology of spiritualities, since they are, in a special manner, subject to the freedom and initiative of the Spirit with his seven gifts and innumerable charismata, the means he uses to make known the fullness of the Son and the life of the Trinity.

This variety in unity is, as Adrienne von Speyr has shown in such bold terms in her commentary on the Apocalyse,[1] the basic meaning of the glorious structure of the heavenly Jerusalem with its twelve gates of different but equally precious stones. They are but gates, however, and therefore ways, modes of access, to something that lies beyond. They

[1] Einsiedeln 1950, 720–759. See also *The Word*, New York 1952.

lead, when traversed in love, to relationships, crossroads, fields, figures, a whole spiritual geometry of heaven, all the constituents of the life of love, for whose furtherance the differences were intended and designed. What will later be manifest in vision can be experienced on earth in faith animated by love, and it is love that, fundamentally, permits (though often hidden from the individual himself) an intimate communication between the different missions and functions and their spirituality. This, however, applies only to genuine spirituality, that which is given as a grace from the Lord. This gives us our best criterion of what constitutes a true ecclesiastical spirituality. It is one which has no element of arbitrary invention, is wholly foreign to any separatism arising from secret feelings of animosity, and does not give itself out as "something special." This is what makes possible a real sharing and communication between spiritual ways.

To make this absolutely clear, we may recall how the great saints, when they came in contact with one another (whether in the body or only in the spirit) not only recognized and understood each other immediately, but entered into community with one another in their different missions. And in all this, the special and particularized mission of each was a means of enabling him to understand, at the deepest level, the other equally special and distinctive mission, and to participate in it. The only thing which faith animated by love finds alien and inaccessible is something itself untrue, which has no inward sphere; for it is this inward sphere which is important, not any outward resemblances there may be. A pure contemplative can enter, with no difficulty, into an intimate Christian communion with one given over to the active life; and likewise a married person with one

107

vowed to virginity. This is possible insofar as the special characteristics of each derive from the grace of the Holy Spirit, their living source. It is at this level they can meet, and not at the level of deliberate reflection and analysis, bringing out points of resemblance or difference. No mission, and no spirituality, is capable of being defined in its living center. They all come from the infinite variety of the divine life, which always exceeds the compass of the human mind. Ultimately, then, we cannot project the geometry of heaven on to the earthly plane, or draw up a system of spirituality. Nor are we required to take our stand on what differentiates one from another in living our own special life, but, forgetting ourselves, to look together on the One who is above us all, that "we be transformed into the same image from glory to glory, as by the Spirit of the Lord" (2 Cor 3:18).

ACTION AND CONTEMPLATION

The history of this classical pair of concepts, when it comes to be written, will assuredly be of the most bewildering complexity; chiefly because, while here in particular, Christian tradition has absorbed much of the Greek culture, it has used the same words sometimes in the ancient Greek sense, and sometimes in a new Christian sense. It was only after a considerable time that it freed itself from the ancient order of ideas, and let itself be guided solely by revelation as to the content and mutual relations of the two concepts.

It is well to begin by distinguishing different levels of meaning, and to bear always in mind that the antithesis between action and contemplation does not belong to the deeper levels of philosophical or theological speculation; the two concepts cannot be precisely demarcated and opposed like those of *actio* and *passio*. The antithesis is, in fact, on a more superficial level, that of daily life, in which the two forms, that of external activity and that of the spiritual attitude which it, at its best, presupposes, can be clearly distinguished. On this level, action means simply external activity,[1] in fact activity restricted to meeting the needs of

[1] *Exterior actio:* S. Th. II, II, 179, 2.

the present life[1] where the spirit has to serve external aims and purposes that will not be present in the life to come.[2] Contemplation, on the other hand, is occupation[3] with the truth for its own sake, and insofar as it is beyond time; ultimately divine truth and everything that stands in relation to it.[4] Thus the pair of concepts are not far removed from the modern concepts of *homo faber* and *homo sapiens,* provided that we rule out all ideological value judgments and evolutionary background; and this corresponds with the different approaches of Plato and Aristotle as developed in the history of ideas, and with the sociological antithesis of σοφός and βάναυσος. It is well to bring out this merely external contrast, which was the starting point of ancient and medieval speculative thought, before examining it at the deeper levels, where the opposition is more doubtful.

1

The meaning given by the ancients to the two concepts and their account of the relationships involve, of necessity, a value judgment, which makes it very difficult to deal with them. The judgment takes explicit form with the subordination of action to contemplation. The purely spiritual occupations in which truth is contemplated and sought for itself alone (in the *artes liberales*) is held superior to those producing things necessary or useful to life, where man's spiritual faculties serve what is material (in the *artes*

---

[1] *Omnia studia humanarum actionum, si ordinentur ad necessitatem praesentis vitae secundum rationem rectam, pertinent ad vitam activam: ibid.* ad 3.

[2] *Ibid.,* 181, 4; I, II, 67, 1 ad 2; 68, 6 ad 3.

[3] *Studium: ibid.,* II, II, 179, 2 ad 3.   [4] *Ibid.,* 180, 3.

serviles); activity directed to truth for its own sake is superior to action for the sake of others, for the common good.

There is a certain danger in accepting this evaluation, since it involves two distinct things. In one aspect, it emphasizes the superiority of the activity of the spirit, which has its end in itself, against that which enslaves it to the task of satisfying earthly needs. Certainly nothing is more necessary in these days than to emphasize the former as the inalienable right and true worth of man as opposed to the despotism of the industrial process which claims the services even of the contemplative as engaged in "mental work." Josef Pieper, in a masterly study,[1] reiterates the old truth, pointing out that regimentation of the mind would most certainly prove fatal to it. "In a logically constructed work-state there can neither be genuine philosophy—since its essence is not to be at the disposal of anyone for his purposes, and so, in this sense, free—nor any science pursued in a philosophical manner, that is, any academic culture in the original sense of the word." The superiority of contemplation to action, in this sense, is one of the inalienable bases not only of classical culture, but of western culture, indeed of any human culture at all.

But closely connected with this is the other aspect of the Greek view: the superiority of what is inner and personal to what is external and social, of *actio immanens* to *actio transiens,* of the act directed to what is above man, the divine and external,[2] to that concerned with the earthly and human, even for the relief of misery and want. It is this

---

[1] *Leisure, the Basis of Culture,* New York 1952.
[2] *Vita contemplativa non proprie humana, sed superhumana.* Q.disp. de virt. card. 1.

111

second aspect that is echoed by Thomas when he ranks those external actions that flow from contemplation, such as teaching and preaching, higher than those "consisting wholly in external matters, such as alms-giving, hospitality, etc.";[1] and, on the other hand, when making a somewhat forced correspondence between the love of God and contemplation, and between the love of one's neighbor and action, he makes the former more meritorious than the latter.[2] Only, as it were, *per accidens* "can it happen that one may merit more in the works of the active life than in those of the contemplative life; for example, when, through his abundance of divine love and for the fulfillment of God's will, one endures, for God's glory, separation for a time from the sweetness of divine contemplation" to devote oneself to action. These judgments are more Hellenic in tone than Christian, and indeed the eight reasons Thomas puts forward for the superiority of contemplation to action are taken entirely from Aristotle, though he subjoins to each an example from the Bible.[3] What is quite plain is that Greece provided not only the categories, but to a great extent also their interpretation and relative assessment. This is true both of Thomas and of the fathers, and in some cases, even more explicitly of the fathers.

With Clement and Origen the Christianization of these two concepts was comparatively successful, since the Christian "gnostic" was represented as not one-sidedly contemplative, but—though with strong emphasis on the intellectual side—as the complete Christian in whom action and con-

---

[1] S. Th. II, II, 188, 6. [2] *Ibid.*, 182, 2.
[3] S. Th. II, II, 182, 1.

templation are joined in harmony. On the other hand, the monastic theology, which reached its peak with Evagrius, forged a system quite inconsonant with Christianity, a super-hellenic system in which the active life (*praktike*) served only as means and prelude to the contemplation of God in the world (*theoria physike*) and, ultimately, of God alone (*theologike*). This exercised a decisive influence on Cassian and Gregory the Great, and they and their disciples only freed themselves from it by degrees and with great trouble. It should be remembered that Augustine, Pope Gregory, even the Cappadocian Gregories, regarded contemplation as pure pleasure, and action as pure affliction—the life they had to suffer, a burden under which they labored, though always looking for respite, and still more for its final cessation. The same attitude persisted, essentially, down to Thomas who, weighted down by so constant a tradition, found it hard to restore, if only in some degree, the Christian balance. As so often with him, it was a balance between different epochs, a summing up of what had gone before with a view into what was to come. While using the ideas and language of tradition, he imperceptibly changed the emphasis, introducing new perspectives and opening the way to future changes.

The accepted formula "contemplation above action" ceased to be so rigidly interpreted with the coming of the mendicant orders, with their ideal of a life in which contemplation flowed out into action, this latter still persisting. Only the action which "*ex plenitudine contemplationis derivatur*"[1] is "to be preferred to simple contemplation.

[1] *Ibid.*, 188, 6.

113

For, just as it is a greater thing to illuminate than merely to shine, so it is greater to communicate what is contemplated than merely to contemplate." The Fathers had virtually apportioned the active and contemplative life between those in the secular and those in the religious life respectively; the Glossa, in fact, comments on the enumeration of the commandments with the words *"ecce vita activa,"* and on the counsel *"si vis perfectus esse . . ."* with *"ecce vita contemplativa."*[1] But Thomas shows that the highest form of Christian mission, the apostolate, is part of the active life, and that the apostles needed the counsels precisely for the perfection of their active work;[2] though (showing how powerful the Greek tradition was) he concludes by saying: "One does not need to stay in the world for the sake of being exercised in the active life; for, even in the religious state, one can practice the active life as much as is needed for initiation and progress in the contemplative."

Side by side with the purely upward movement characteristic of the patristic age, room is now found for the movement of descent—hesitatingly, at first, but more and more confidently as Christian inferences came into play. The statement that "the higher reason, destined for contemplation, is related to the lower, directed to action, as husband to wife, since she has to be guided by him"[3] certainly indicates superiority of the former to the latter. But perhaps we may take the image more seriously, and ask whether man must not turn to woman in order to be fruitful, must not pass through "the gate of humiliation and death" (in Claudel's words) to prove his virility? Is not the wife "the glory of her

[1] *Contra retr.* c 2.   [2] *Ibid.,* c 7 ad 7.
[3] S. Th. II, II, 182, 4.

husband"? Furthermore the movement of descent is, surely, the movement of revelation, on which it places particular emphasis. After all, the time Christ passed in contemplation was a preparation for his time of action; and the time of his vision of the Father was the preparation for the supreme moment, decisive for the world's redemption, of the "non-vision," the "My God, why have you forsaken me?" In fact, this obscurity of his must be held to be the fulfillment of the Son's contemplation in his earthly state; therein the *contemplata aliis tradere* was carried to the point of total renunciation, emptying, kenosis of contemplation in action carried to its utmost extreme, when action ends by becoming passion. All kinds of considerations are suggested here, which, while they do not invalidate the old conception, show that, as formulated, it bears only on a comparatively superficial aspect of the problem.

2

The problem is approached on a deeper level by Aquinas when he bases the concepts of the active and contemplative life on the more general concepts of the two dispositions, the active productive, on the one hand, and the contemplative receptive, on the other. And since he derives these explicitly from the two basic dispositions of the intellect,[1] the problem merges into that of the relations between these two. Now, however, it becomes at once apparent that contemplation is far from being mere passive reception; it is an act in which *actio* and *passio* are combined, and, in another

---

[1] *Activum et contemplativum, sive speculativum et practicum, sunt differentiae intellectus. Ibid.*, 179, 1, obj. 2.

aspect, the highest activity of the created spirit. Thomas was fully conscious of this paradox of the creature, namely that the more it is receptive to God, the more it participates in his activity,[1] so that, as the power of contemplation increases, so does that of action; in fact, the highest act of the spirit, intellectual vision, is always described (with Aristotle) as *operatio,* though it is also (as Augustine maintained) reception of the absolute Object.

From this it follows that the distinction between the two kinds of life is wholly a human one, and valid only for human life on earth; consequently, it is no more than provisional. For the angels there is no distinction between action and contemplation.[2] Likewise with Adam there was no opposition between the two; his action meant no interruption to his contemplation.[3] The opposition only arose when, through sin, activity became a hindrance, a disturbance to contemplation.[4] In the saints, who had overcome the source of this hindrance, the former unity, at least in some degree, is restored, the unity which, present in angels and men untainted by sin, reflected the design of the Creator. And just as the angels, when engaged in their active mission, never lose the vision of God,[5] so must the perfect man be capable of regaining the original state of harmony.

The whole problem of the nature of truth, which is both theoretical and practical, points in the same direction. Here we can only give some indications of its complexity. Truth, contemplated and received, is also active, and this in two respects: first, as the immanent act of the spirit, both in the

---

[1] *Quanto aliqua natura Deo vicinior, tanto minus ab eo inclinatur et nata est seipsam inclinare.* De Ver. 22, 4.

[2] S. Th. II, II, 181, 4 ad 2. [3] *Ibid.,* I, 94, 1.

[4] *Ibid.,* II, II, 181, 4 ad 2. [5] Greg., Mor. I, 2 c. 2.

process of discursive reasoning and in intellectual vision—
there can be no intellect without will,[1] will and intellect
presuppose each other[2]—secondly, a direct consequence of
this, because truth must be acted upon as well as perceived.
This is the true sense of the existential character of truth;
we only really possess it, when we do it; it has not only to
be grasped and seen in concepts, but expressed in the whole
of one's being and life. This leads on at once to John's
"*facere veritatem*" (Jn 3:21), and he certainly is not to be
suspected of activism. Something of the kind is expressed
by Thomas when he points out that many acts belong equally
to the active and contemplative life, and are explained in
terms of each. Thus prudence, in the strict sense, is one of
the moral virtues, which pertain to the active life, but in the
wider sense it pertains to the contemplative;[3] and if the
active virtues are seen as preparing the way for the contemplative, they too belong to the contemplative life.[4] Consequently the two dispositions, contemplative and active,
though one may be more pronounced in a given case than
the other, form part of a deeper unity. They condition each
other mutually, as do intellect and will, between which there
exists a reciprocal priority, contemplation being a prerequisite of true action,[5] and action the indispensable condition of
true contemplation.[6] The highest point of attainment is a
unity wherein action occurs not—as is often the danger—to
the detriment of contemplation,[7] but as its fulfillment; much
as the Church is the fullness of Christ, not that she adds

[1] S. Th. I, 16, 4.   [2] *Ibid.*, ad obj.
[3] *Ibid.*, II, II, 181, 2.   [4] *Ibid.*, 181, 1 ad 3.
[5] *Ibid.*, 181, 1 ad 1.   [6] *Ibid.*, 181, 1 ad 2.
[7] Per modum subtractionis: *ibid.*, 182, 1 ad 3.

anything, but provides the sphere for this fullness to spread abroad, make itself known and work its effect.

Thomas admits no exclusiveness in the choice of vocations. There may well be a natural propensity, in various cases, more to action or to contemplation, but those more suited to the active life can, by their active work, be schooled to contemplation, and those attracted to the contemplative life may take on the work of the active life in order to fit themselves better for contemplation.[1]

3

So far we have not reached the core of the problem, but have remained on the philosophical level. To do so, we must go direct to revelation, making it the ultimate criterion, and if any previous conclusions fail to withstand the test, they must be discarded without hesitation.

1. What is of greatest significance here is the example of Christ, whose life exhibits a whole network of relationships between contemplation and action. As to his inner disposition, what we may call the background of his soul, it was always a constant, uninterrupted unity of both. Just as the Trinity is ever at rest and at work, ever beholds itself and continues the missions within the Godhead, so is the soul of Christ ever occupied with the vision of the Father and carrying out his mission: "The Son cannot do anything . . . but what he sees the Father doing" (Jn 5:19). Christ's contemplation consists in his being the Word of the *Father,* his action in his being the *Word* of the Father. "I speak that which I have seen with my Father" (Jn 8:38). The fact

[1] *Ibid.* 4 ad 3.

that his own witness is a double witness expresses the unity, grounded in the Trinity, of action and contemplation. Because it is so grounded, it is no dead sameness, but an expression of the most intense life, of the divine life, which can only be translated into human terms in Christ's life by the temporal interaction of the two poles. So it is that his whole life consists in thirty years of contemplation and three of action, these in turn opening with the forty days of contemplation. Furthermore he devotes his days to action, his nights to contemplation, drawing, by his action, the disciples and the people more and more deeply into his contemplation, making them see that his action is simply the expression of his contemplation. The whole time of the Lord on earth can be considered action that flows from the fullness of his heavenly and eternal contemplation, and returns to it. It can also be seen as flowing from his heavenly and eternal action, which consists in doing the Father's will in eternity—in fact, to be the infinite expression of this will, the Father's will personified; and so both his eternal contemplation and his temporal action and contemplation can be seen as serving his eternal action. He is the perfect unity of action and passive acceptance; he is generated by the Father and, at the same time, he makes fully his own this generative act. The sole measure for both his action and contemplation is his absolute love for the Father; whatever proceeds from this love is perfect and unsullied. His descent into the world is something as perfect as his abiding with the Father; his love for his fellowmen as perfect as that for his Father. Nor is his action on earth any less perfect than his contemplation in heaven.

In the light of this, whatever remains of Greek intellec-

119

tualism in Thomas must be abandoned. It is no solution of the problem to assign the love of God to contemplation and the love of one's neighbor to action, and to subordinate the latter to the former.[1] The love spoken of in 1 Cor 13 is as much love for God as for one's neighbor, equally active and contemplative. Again, it is useless to assign the intellectual vision of what is above man (whereby man is associated with God and the angels) to contemplation and to assign concern for earthly things by the *ratio inferior* (whereby man is associated with the animals) to action,[2] something which need obliges us to endure.[3] For if this descent to a lower level really occurs *propter abundantiam divini amoris, ut ejus voluntas impleatur, propter ipsius gloriam,* and if this was clearly Christ's way, any contrary value judgment is clearly false, all previous ideas of relative importance must give way to the normative movement of Christ himself.

This is all the more imperative in that, as we have seen already, Christ's action and contemplation, inseparable as they are, issue finally in the passion, which, as the ultimate aim (*telos;* Jn 13:1) of his earthly life, was likewise that of his action and contemplation. The passion was the immanent end of his action, since all his works and achievements lead logically to their climax in the voluntary sacrifice of his life (Jn 10:18). Thus it is that his passion is the culmination of his action, his weakness the culmination of his strength, his final impotence the most striking expression of his omnipotence, his failure the moment of his highest achievement. And the Eucharist, which makes permanent his self-giving for the world, is what universalizes his action

[1] *Ibid.* II, II, 182:1.
[3] *Ibid.* II, II, 182, 2.
[2] *Ibid.* I, II, 3, 5; II, II, 182, 1.

in the Church, formerly bound by temporal restrictions. The passion is equally the end of his contemplation, inasmuch as the latter was his abiding disposition to let the Father's will work in him. Because his action finally becomes the passion, he shows the world that the former was always a form of his contemplation, that the Father was in him, spoke by him, and worked the works that he did. And since his contemplation becomes, in the passion, the night of not-seeing, it is also the culmination of human contemplation, where God prevails so much that even the sight of his light is destroyed by that very light, that summit is reached that is described by the Areopagite as "dazzling darkness," of which the perfect example was that experienced on the cross. Here again the Eucharist is the culmination and perpetuation of his contemplation on the cross, since in it he continues to pour himself forth, always ready to give himself completely.

2. Christ's attitude is the model for the Christian, for whom Christ, and no other, is the standard. The Christian is, in the first place, Mary, who in contrast with Christ as God and man represents the unity of action and contemplation in a pure creature. At the same time, she incarnates the feminine form of this unity, as distinct from the masculine form of the Son, though he too prefigures the feminine form, insofar as everything in the created order is receptive in relation to God. Both as a woman and as a creature, and also (as Scheeben says) as the archetype of the Church, contemplation is her chief concern; her cooperation consists in acceptance, holding herself in readiness as the vessel of the Word. Her action, therefore, itself has a pronounced contemplative character. Over and above this, she completes, as woman and helper, the work of her Son as man.

121

During the time of her contemplation, she is intensely active, in order to foster her contemplation; during the time of her action, she is intent on contemplation, so that prayer may accompany her action. Only in the passion, when all distinction and priority as to action and contemplation finally disappear, does her hour and that of the Son coincide perfectly.

The creature's readiness to receive God's word differs from that of Christ in that, for the former, the word is always something far beyond his comprehension, impossible to measure, and to be received only in the obedience of faith. Man's response to it must be a readiness to let God ceaselessly widen and expand his spirit for the reception of the word. This is especially the case for those whose vocation it is to preach and interpret the word of God in the Church. But should anyone think that he has understood sufficiently for himself or for others, or be content with the ideas he has worked out as adequate for his work "for the time being," he misconceives the essence of the word, its divinity and transcendence of all human ideas, and so cannot any longer speak of it in a Christian way. The only person whose witness sounds credible is one whose audience feels that he speaks from a sense of "the charity of Christ which surpasses all knowledge" (Eph 3:18).

While the Christian life ostensibly consists in alternate periods of action and contemplation, its aim should be to make the two interpenetrate more and more. With the saints they were no longer distinguishable. The saint in his activities can be in a perfect state of contemplation. In the sick whom he serves he sees Christ; in his obedience he sees and makes his own the grace of Christ's obedience; and so, in the

formula of Ignatius, he can be *in actione contemplativus.*
Furthermore he does not himself decide the extent of his
action and of his contemplation, so as not to incur the risk
of losing his contemplation in an excess of action; nor does
he consider that intensification of action assures him a
corresponding advance in contemplation. He is always conscious that the formula *in actione contemplativus* itself presupposes the ancient patristic and Thomistic *ex abundantia
contemplationis activus.* Above all, he guards himself from
the attempt to mark out the effective range of his action,
which, in any case, is fed by contemplation, itself not limited
in its effects. The fruit of Christian action, since it is a
divine fruit, always goes beyond its visible range. It comes,
therefore, in part within the sphere of contemplation, just as
the fruit of contemplation itself is action not always perceptible to the contemplative. This is what we now have,
finally, to consider.

3. The fathers and the scholastics were unable to develop
fully a Christian doctrine of contemplation and action, because they shared with the Greek philosophers a too indi-
vidualistic idea of contemplation, and so failed to see where
its real fruitfulness lay. Thomas, along with all who pre-
ceded him, saw fruitfulness as preeminently due to action,
and action, therefore, as that which makes contemplation
fruitful.[1] But the contemplation which is concerned with
God alone he held to be a purely individual affair. Though
he placed the *religio mixta* above the purely contemplative,
he made the *vita eremitica* higher than the *vita socialis,*
since "the perfect man is sufficient to himself," however
much the *vita socialis* was necessary to bring him to this

[1] S. Th. II, II, 188, 6.

123

perfection.[1] It is astonishing how long it took for men to see that this self-sufficient perfection, to be Christian, must be, in a mysterious sense, a life fruitful for the Church, radiating out into the apostolate. The lack of this perception makes the arguments of the fathers and scholastics for the superiority of contemplation not fully convincing. De Guibert had reason to be surprised that even Suarez seems to have had hardly any inkling of the significance of contemplation for the apostolate. Admittedly the fruit of contemplation cannot be assessed in the terms of this world. That part of it that Thomas saw, the effect on teaching and preaching, is only a small one. The greater part of it remains hidden in the mystery of God's action, in the invisible action of grace over the entire Church, indeed the whole of mankind. And it is just because the contemplative renounces any vision of his fruits that his action is so widespread, pouring out like a river into the limitless sea of God's infinite action, flowing too into the inexhaustible treasury of the Church and, in consequence, of greater social and communal significance than anything else. The pure contemplative, as Teresa of Lisieux said, completely renounces not only material, but also spiritual possessions. Her autobiography culminates in an apothlosis of the power of contemplation. She calls it the Archimedean point from which the world can be raised up; it sends to God flowers which, when gathered by the Church triumphant and passed through the Lord's hands, "receive immeasurable value," "are strewn over the Church suffering, to extinguish her flames, and over the Church militant to ensure her victory." The condition for this, she repeats, is that the contemplative renounce seeing the fruit for himself;

[1] *Ibid.*, 188, 8.

that, with the contemplative and eucharistic Lord, he be wholly intent on transmitting it; that he desire nothing more than "to be a ray proceeding from the forehead of my mother," the Church.

The fruitfulness of pure contemplation is not a privilege reserved to it alone, but points to what is ultimately the sole source of fruitfulness both of action and contemplation: charity. We may here substitute for "fruitfulness" the word "meritoriousness" (which, however, is narrower than the former), and then this same truth is expressed in the statement: *efficacia et radix meriti est caritas*—the efficacy and root of merit is charity.[1] But charity "seeks not her own" (1 Cor 13:5); it does not aim at "accumulating merits" for oneself, but at giving the fruits it bears to God and the Church—fruits of its contemplative action or active contemplation. "Do not lay in stores. Distribute the goods as soon as they are received. Even if you live to be eighty years old, remain poor. Learn how to avoid saving up, give all you have back again at once" (Teresa of Lisieux).

[1] S. Th. I, II, 114, 4; II, II, 182, 2.

For many Catholics, Christian thinking reached its final, glorious consummation with Thomas Aquinas; and, likewise, for many Protestants the world begins with Luther. Should they chance to wander awhile outside the enclosure of the Reformation, it is for the sake of showing that all roads lead to Wittenberg, that the middle ages were Pelagian, the patristic era Neoplatonist, and Irenaeus already a papist. They fully subscribe to Claudel's passage: "Of none of the saints was it written that he was necessary, but Luther *had* to come" (*The Satin Slipper*, fifth day, scene 1); and, further, they consider him the key to Church history. For if the Reformation, with the separation from Rome, had not been necessary, the bough on which they sit would be extremely precarious. The division of the Church is axiomatic to Protestant thought of whatever complexion. Catholic thought, on the contrary, presupposes that the division was not necessary, that if both sides think deeply and widely enough and in the spirit of obedience, agreement can and must be reached, and that Protestantism, which the Catholic Church is obliged to describe as heretical, is yet, ultimately and seen in the light of its origins, only a schism.

Catholics are compelled to this view by obedience to the

God of the Old and New Testaments, to whose command
the splitting of the Church is diametrically opposed. Whatever justification for it may be proposed on the ground of
historical or philosophical necessity, none can be adduced
from theology or purely Christian considerations. We should
meditate long and seriously on the lapidary sentences of
Karl Barth which I put at the beginning of my study of him;
in them he brands as an act of disobedience any attempt to
derive a plurality of churches from the New Testament
(*Theol. Existenz* 27, 6ff.). Plurality is not to be treated
otherwise than as an effect of sin, and that means, primarily,
for each person, his own sin. And this is intensified whenever one of the contestants presupposes as a maxim that
there must be separate churches. There is, in fact, in a
Christian view, no such necessity. Even the plea "I cannot
see it otherwise" will not excuse a person before the eternal
judge. Our guilt before world history is immeasurable; for,
when the quarrels between Christian bodies destroy the
unity of Christ's Church, the unity intended as the living
proof of his commandment, then its witness to the world of
the power of love is simply a mockery. In place of Christianity we now have "confessions," whose essence it is to
stress mainly the "anti," at least for psychological (the
Catholics) if not theological (for Protestants) reasons. As
a result, they become, in practice, useless for the mission
incumbent on Christianity at all times, now more than ever:
to offer the principle of a unity to the world and its history
that transcends all their differences. "But if the salt lose its
savor, wherewith shall it be salted?"; and this applies not
only to the salt, but to those who should be salted. For the
truth is that the Christian with his claim to bring all minds

into the captivity of Christ is irritating enough to men, but he becomes intolerable when, by making subtle distinctions, he produces additional bonds to lay on them.

Some may claim that the Christian message, especially in these days, can only commend itself as reflecting the spirit of its founder if it is made clear that its prohibitions derive from a fundamental and comprehensive affirmation, such as accords both with theology and with practical needs and the human disposition; accords, that is to say, both with all the Christian confessions and with the religious, ethical and philosophical attitudes of mankind in general, without on that account countenancing anything inconsistent with Christianity. In short, it should exhibit itself as one—perhaps the best, the highest—offshoot of the common stem of natural and human religion as evidenced throughout history. This, in fact, is the course taken by liberalism of every stamp; and anyone who adopts it is sure of the applause of all non-Christians, who quite legitimately seek the unity of religion in that of human nature and its universal quest for God.

The opposite extreme is that of those who, in the name of the unity of Christ, condemn this attempt at unity on theological grounds or even regard it as a rampart erected against Christ and the preachers of the truth, and therefore to be battered down. There remains only the middle way, according to which unity is given from above, precisely because it is absolute and not *prima inter pares religiones,* as what fundamentally—even in the midst of crises and conflicts, and, when they must come, upheavals—evinces itself as affirming, embodying and fulfilling all human needs and aspirations. This attitude may be called a "universalism

129

from above, meaning that the "peak," which is God's revelation in Christ and its proclamation, is not the outcome of the "base," the world and human nature, but is the peak *of* the base (or *above* the base), which is all it can be; the more so, in fact, in that it refers itself to the base, and for its sake has come into being as revelation. Those who cry alarm at this attitude on the ground that the relationship envisaged is "dangerous" and slippery, that those who adopt it will be swept away by the undertow (of the "base"), of which there are numerous examples in the history of theology, are right in their warning, but not in their attempt to prohibit it. The Church's transcendence over the world is given in advance, it is not a resultant of other causes. Therefore theology also transcends philosophy, and cannot do without it, since all human thought is *Weltanschauung,* "philosophy." Anyone who fails to realize this will fall into both extremes. He will first set theology alongside philosophy, and so, willy-nilly, hold it as one *Weltanschauung* among others; and then protest against this confusion, and, in combating it, withdraw into an isolationist position.

It would be hard to acquit the historical phenomenon known as dialectical theology of partial guilt for the disruption of German philosophy. Doubtless, the more rabid "dialecticians" would rejoice at this, since they consider German philosophy to be a secularization and degeneration of orthodox Protestantism, and that a *tabula rasa* would be better than this ignominy. But the consequence of this, among the more alert of the younger theologians, has been a feeling of suffocation in a prison of their own choosing, of having lost contact with the age, of unreality. This, in turn,

130

has led to an attempt at escape into the old Bismarckian regimentation of the Church, or into individual skirmishes in the no man's land between orthodoxy and liberalism (demythologizing), as if "fresh air" could be expected from there. This is not the way to regain contact with actual history, nor will it come through endless talk about "historicity." The only way is by a resolute change in the inmost heart; to eschew quarrelsomeness in favor of an open Catholic attitude, in the best sense of that expression, that is, free of suspiciousness, ready to credit others with the best intentions. There must be the conviction that, since history in the Old Testament right up to its culmination in the incarnation played such a theological role, it is only right that it should do so in the time of the Church, when the "body" is growing up—and this implies a temporal, historical dimension—to the fullness of age already attained by Christ, the Head. God came not to judge history, but to save it. Still less is such judgment incumbent on the theologian, whose attitude should be one of affirmation, blessing it with the benediction of God. Indeed this is the only Christian approach.

Karl Barth's keen interest in history, even secular history, political and economic, is well known. It would, however, be a mistake for us to consider it merely an occupation for his leisure; it is, in fact, all part of his work as theologian. The study of the Bible and that of secular history, when pursued in an open, receptive spirit, do not result in two separate views of reality. Admittedly it is not accorded us to construct a "synthesis" of the two, a theology of history, for we know that the synthesis, the full unity, subsists in Christ. So we are careful not to make its study serve our conceptions— whether those of the Reformation or of our own favored

131

dogmatic system! Instead, we allow it to lead up to him in whom takes place "the restitution of all things, which God has spoken by the mouth of his holy prophets, from the beginning of the world" (Acts 3:21).

In Karl Barth we meet with a Protestantism which, in contrast with the dogmatism of many of his disciples, has the power to reach beyond the sphere of controversy, and to regain a genuine Christian universalism. Though he makes no concession to liberalism (which, of course, can be "universal" and conciliatory, but only through abandoning the difference between "peak" and "base"), yet in him for the first time Protestant theology seems to have attained an inner catholicity of the theological reason, and so to have engaged in a real dialogue with the *Weltanschauungen*. For Karl Barth the history of the Church of Christ begins not with the Reformation, but with Christ. The main point of his exposition of Luther is that his real function was to bring about a reform of certain essential doctrines within the one *Corpus christianum,* whereas his "founding a church" was a mistake with tragic consequences. The most significant positive part of Barth's work is his doctrine of predestination and his eschatology so closely bound up with it. Here, in the most crucial points, he parts company with Calvin. He gives the primacy to christology, even as regards God's original decree of creation, and thereby frees his teaching completely from the Protestant ethos that, more than anything else at the present time, hinders the propagation of the Gospel, now that the world has become conscious of its unity. The outer coat he strips off was not due, in the first place, to the Reformation, though strengthened by it, but much more, though not exclusively, to the early and

132

high middle ages. Its real origin was Augustine and his doctrine of the last things, not a dialectical but a dualistic doctrine. Its formal structure seems to have remained with Augustine from his eleven years of Manichaeism, and to have been so much a part of his mind that it patently affected even his last controversial writings, quite apart from its more hidden workings, as in the general plan of the *Civitas Dei*. It gave rise to a grim doctrine of predestination, which was taken up, in an almost slavish spirit, by succeeding generations. What they lacked in particular was an historical and philological outlook which would have enabled them to have brought out the true import, dialectical and eschatological, of the ideas and terminology of the two testaments, instead of interpreting them cosmologically. It was Augustine who spoke the words *"territus terreo"* (*Sermo* 40, c.3; *PL* 38:246), and his fears prevented him from seeing, despite his genius, "how his constant referring to the tension between mercy and justice meant putting this tension in the place of the sovereign God and of God's love, which, according to the great passage in the epistle to the Romans, is the sole ultimate factor, for 'God hath concluded all in unbelief, that he may have mercy on all.' "[1]

Karl Barth, in going back beyond Augustine and the influence he had on the whole official theology up to Calvin, finds himself unexpectedly in the field of pre-Augustine patrology, and is confronted with its most powerful thinker, one who, through his universalism, has affected, more than anyone else, his own and subsequent generations. Anyone who approaches the great Alexandrian with unbiased mind, and compares him with Barth, while allowing for the obvi-

[1] Przywara, *Augustinus, Die Gestalt als Gefüge,* Hegner 1934, 111.

133

ous differences and the centuries that separate them, will be struck at once by their affinity. Origen, of course, thought in a Hellenistic environment, his idea of the world was gnostic, his psychology Stoic and Platonist, he adhered to the allegorism of Philo, as well as, though less explicitly, to current ideas of the same sort. All this, however, does not constitute the real object of his impassioned thought, nor, in consequence, the original and captivating quality of his theology.[1]

We are indebted to Origen and Karl Barth for the two most coherent outlines of a theology of the Word, the Word that is the eternal Son of the Father—not, however the *Logos nudus*, but *incarnandus* and *incarnatus*. It is he who upholds the creation and is its justification, and, in his historical revelation, finally embodied in Scripture, evinces himself as the ultimate meaning of the whole creation and as the revelation of the Father inherent in it from the beginning. It would be a misunderstanding of Origen's basic position to subordinate the incarnation of the Logos to a universal, neutral presence of him in every created reason. This presence is indeed affirmed in that Origen has no conception of reason except as the organ for hearing the Word, and he expounds the words "In the midst of you there stands one whom you know not" in the sense of the presence (parousia) of the Logos in the midst of every man's reason. At the same time, his attitude to the heretical and

[1] There is hardly any account of his work that does full justice to his central thesis. One may consult A. Lieske, *Die Theologie der Logosmystik bei Origenes* (1938), my "Mysterion d'Origène," *Revue des sciences religieuses,* XXVI/XXVII 1936/37, and *Origenes: Geist und Feuer* (1954), and especially de Lubac: *Histoire et Esprit. L'intelligence de l'Ecriture d'après Origène,* Aubier 1950.

non-Christian sects and philosophies makes it quite plain that he had no intention of subordinating the historical revelation of the Word to a general, neutral one. He saw the latter at most as provisional and preparatory, or else something obscure and distorted, from which it was possible to learn a little, particularly in the way of philosophical or dialectical exposition, but always recalling the Christian thinker, who should profit by them, to his own special heritage (*spolia Aegyptiorum*). For him the center of world history is the process of redemption, to which he devotes unremittingly all the energies of his mind. As described in the Bible, it presents three elements, which he precisely delineates: the inseparableness (if not complete identity) of the Logos as Christ, God and man, and the Logos as Scripture, which is essentially a manifestation of Christ (the letter as "body" and "sacrament" of the Word); though he never equates the letter—behind which the exegete can never go for the sake of grasping the naked sense or event—with the Logos-person. The second element is the inner mutual relationship of universalism and divine election in the economy of salvation, a tension which, for Karl Barth, is solved only by the idea of social representation on the one hand (for Origen, as a Catholic, the idea too of co-representation on the part of Christ's disciples: the apostles and the "gnostics" or "saints," who pray, combat, sacrifice themselves for the Church and mankind), and by Paul's idea of grace ever outweighing guilt (Rom 5), on the other. The history of salvation, decided once and for all, is prolonged in the individual's decisions for himself and self-commitment.

Finally, the third element, closely bound up with the

135

others, is one strongly emphasized by Origen—the contemporaneous character of revelation, of the Word as here and now proceeding from the Father. It means the continuing demand that we, as persons, should encounter the Word as a person, go beyond the "letter" and comprehend and fulfill it as "spirit." It is this characteristic which imparts to the whole of Origen's theology a dynamism enabling it to penetrate through every external covering, every rite, institution and outward historical circumstance to the spiritual truth, so that he almost comes to view as merely phenomenal the outer envelope of "flesh," "letter," "sacrament" and "institution." Yet it is the same dynamism that, if we abstract from confessional differences, we find in Karl Barth. Now it is this dynamism, and not a gnostic preconception foreign to the Bible, that enables Origen, more adequately than any of his successors, to grasp the double aspect of the revealed word in its "existential dialectic" of judgment and grace, both in the Old Testament utterances, especially the prophets, and in the sayings of Christ and their exposition by Paul and John. Origen (as also Karl Barth; see his *Epistle to the Romans*) at first, in the *Peri Archon,* succumbed to the temptation of a "systematic" exposition of this double aspect, and it cost him dear; but, subsequently, he consistently strove to harmonize his treatment with that of Scripture. In other words, his whole aim was to avoid playing down the aspect of judgment in favor of that of grace, while not darkening the picture so much as to minimize the aspect of grace and weaken the force of the words of Paul and John. We cannot just solve the question by the shibboleth "*apokatastasis,*" a term rightly applied to the pantheist systems of later disciples such as Evagrius and Bar Sudaili. They made the Hellenic principle of decline and restoration prevail everywhere, even in the history of salvation; but for Origen, with his scrupulous attention to the words of Scripture, the term had a much more restrained meaning. Apart from a few places outside the *Peri Archon,* he uses a suitably biblical terminology. At most it could be said that he elicits a great deal from a passage in virtue of an implicit preconception, and that many a text, which, read in a different connection, would be lacking in force and color, becomes extraordinarily illuminating, just as the fascinating power of Karl Barth's exegesis in connection with the doctrine of predestination (he himself speaks of a "strange illumination") derives from the same implied supposition.

Yet, since for both the person of Christ, who represents the *autobasileia,* is in his sovereign freedom the judgment and pronounces it, the assertion does not prejudice the future, but remains open and full of hope—which, being a theological virtue, excludes no possibility. They both excel in showing how the twofold aspect of the cross (election joined with reprobation) is reflected in the history of salvation, especially in the relationship of the Jews and Gentiles, of the Old and the New Testaments. It is here that Origen, like the Karl Barth of the second *Epistle to the Romans,* manifests a decided sense of the dialectic, the "hazardous quality" of the election of the individual in the Church (see commentary on Ez 16). Origen, it is true, stresses even more than Barth the agony of the Christian life, the involvement of the spiritual man in the struggle between light and darkness, between Christ and the powers of evil. Yet he is, at the same time, conscious of the inequality of the two opponents, of the ontological nothingness of the evil principle, so strongly emphasized by Barth and given prominence by Origen's successors, Gregory of Nyssa, Maximus, Eriugena. In this context, Origen does more justice to the two aspects, and so to the biblical record, than does Barth in that he takes a graver view of the strength of what is negative and its temptations, and feels that sin—especially that of Christians—is an outrage done to the Logos who, even though glorified, continues (in Pascal's sense) his passion to the end of the world.

This leads us to a highly important topic. It is constantly objected against Barth that his optimistic universalism cannot be brought into harmony with the facts of sin and judgment as presented in such somber terms in both testaments. This objection is not without foundation, in that Barth does not give sufficient weight to certain counterbalancing factors in the Bible, which, however, are quite consistent with his position as already described. It is not enough to adduce the idea (not exclusively biblical, but strongly Neoplatonist) of the essential nothingness of evil, which cannot enter into any real competition with God, and to invoke the great contrast between the state of being with God (heaven, immunity from death) and that of rejection by God (hell, conceived by Thomas as "evil infinity," endless temporality). The counterweight consists in the solemn and momentous character of the words of judgment addressed by the Lord and his apostles and prophets to the sinner, their absoluteness in the sense of transcending all that is temporal and all relationship with time. And it consists, in addition, in the existentiality of theological "science" as such, a property manifested in the (Catholic) "science of the saints," and not foreign to Karl Barth, but yet only

reaching its full development when the (Catholic) grace—
pure grace!—of the Church's participation in Christ's redemptive work is recognized as possible and an actual
reality. The experiences to which John of the Cross gave
the name of the dark night of the spirit, and which are
constantly repeated in the (above all, Roman!) western
Church, keep alive in her a vivid consciousness of how
tremendous and frightful a reality was endured on the cross,
something far beyond what could be described as God's
wrath with and condemnation of a creature. This is the
reason for a certain hesitation in the preaching of the absolute victory of Christ, even with Paul and John, as also for
the agitation pervading Origen's work, and which, down
the centuries, distinguishes, by a fine, hardly perceptible
line, Catholic from Protestant universalism.[1] A danger
which Protestant teaching does not always escape is that of
a certain exhilaration at being redeemed, as extreme as was
the despondency resulting from an obsession with guilt.
Karl Barth's keen sense of theological balance keeps him
free from both these extremes; but lesser minds, claiming
affinity with him, find perhaps in the "tremendous illumination" by which he himself was shaken occasion for mis-

---

[1] ". . . *Denique cupit anathema fieri a Christo pro fratribus suis . . .
Nonne summae amentiae videtur esse, veram Vitam repellere, summam
Sapientiam arguere, Omnipotentiae resistere? Nonne Vitam repellit qui
pro fratribus a Christo separari cupit, sicut et ille qui dicit: "Aut
ignosce illis hanc noxam, aut dele me de libro quem scripsisti?" Nonne
Sapientiam arguere seu velle docere videtur, qui ad Dominum loquitur:
"Absit a te ut hanc rem facias et occidas cum impio justum, fiatque
justus sicut impius" (Gn. 18:25; see Ex 32). Non est tuum hoc, qui
judicas omnem terram, nequaquam facies judicium! Nonne Omnipotentiae resistere tentavit, Omnipotentisque iram mitigare homo prae-
sumpsit atque praevaluit, quando jam egressa sententia a Domino,
quando jam saeviente incendio, igni furenti se objecit? . . ."* Richard of
St. Victor, *De quatuor gradibus violentae caritatis* (PL 196, 1224).

139

placed emphases. How one should speak of a mystery which one must neither ignore nor vulgarize is a permanent question in this life of ours, which always involves a profanation of what is sacred.

Origen was alive to this existential dimension of theology. He expressed it in contemporary language, and, since he had no other terminology to work with, he applied to it the distinction between the *Haplousteroi* and the *Gnostikoi*— implying thereby a certain esoterism, though in typical fashion he did not press it unduly. We can do without these expressions, for what they signify can always be presented in the analogy between those whose knowledge is inward, the effect of grace (the true "theologians," as understood by the fathers, such as Gregory of Nazianzen and the Areopagite), and those who view the mysteries more from the outside, and construct a system about them.

Our intention is not to present the "system" of Origen as obligatory or even as a model for Christian theology. We mention it only as historically the most influential body of thought outside the long period from Augustine to Calvin. In the patristic era there were certainly other theologians who, in their whole work or in considerable parts of it, presented a true Christian universalism in the sense of Karl Barth. In fact, they were not lacking in the middle ages, as we may see from the christocentric theology in the last book of *De Docta Ignorantia* of Nicholas of Cusa.

We can look for a moment on the theme we started with. What we said about "peak" and "base" will be viewed with misgiving by Karl Barth and his followers. It is, once again, the Catholic harmonization of opposites. The concepts of creation and testament are also seen to be in accord; in the last analysis, this means the accord between Father and Son. The readiness of the preacher of the Gospel to accept the thought and philosophy of mankind shows two things. The first is that he has no hesitation in taking in the fullest sense the command "unto all the ends of the earth the Gospel must be preached," that man is to be taken as he is (and this includes his *Weltanschauung,* which necessarily confronts him with God—even in his idolatry!). The second is the conviction that Christ, the victor and Lord of all peoples, is already in the place where the preacher comes, who, therefore, may with perfect rightness look on the alien *Weltanschauung* as already touched with the light of Christ. For God himself has already contemplated the world in that same light, and even before, chronologically speaking, the event of Christ's death.

In this historical situation—and there is simply no other —something more should be said about the meaning of the *analogia entis.* The fundamental openness of Christian teaching to the *thing* (not the word!) is all part of what goes to make up the Catholic idea of Christian (and theological) universalism; in fact, it is the most striking instance of this approach.

1. First, it should be noticed that at the time when the inquiry into being was vigorously pursued, this term was one of God's names, and therefore, *essentially,* not a concept at all. The expression "concept of being" (*conceptus entis*) is a self-contradiction, as every western philosophy worthy of the name will admit. "Openness" to the incomprehensible mystery of being is the transcendental prerequisite for any conceptual structure. The Greek fathers and Augustine took up the position that "natural" reason, by the very fact of

141

being unable to understand *what* God is, and in foregoing any statement about his essence, comes to know *that* he is and is this "is," just because, as eluding understanding (*si comprehendis, non est Deus*), it is experienced as incomparable with all that we experience as being in the context of this world; in relation to this it is "ever more dissimilar." If this "structure," outside of which there is no human thought, is not taken into account, there can be no recognition of the "divine" quality of revelation or that the divine voice "descends" to us from an absolutely transcendent sphere. Karl Barth might reply that only the divine voice itself can make known to us the height from which it descends; otherwise, man could know and measure prior to revelation the distance that separates him and God. This would of course be true if we took *esse* as a concept, as the textbooks do when they deal with analogy, though with the proviso that it is a question "only of an analogous concept." However, in so doing, they forget that the formal ontology they treat of is the *Mysteriun tremendum* of the Godhead, which, while it has decreed from the beginning to speak with the creature, yet betrays by the tone of its voice that it was free to keep eternally silent. It is always possible, and often useful, to protest against the facile nature of textbook formulas; but such protests must always be accompanied by reflection on the subject to which they refer.

2. More positively: *Esse* is a name of God, and not one that we just happened to choose, for it does not signify an "attribute," but indicates the basis of all the attributes. It is a name that applies essentially to him alone, which means that his essence is one with his existence. Consequently we arrive, as we reflect, at the point where we have to renounce

142

thinking of God as something "other," as an object apart from us. He is the universality of being—as Sir 43:29 says, and it is, therefore, evident that he is a partner in a two-sided relationship that, as a relationship of I to Thou, seems of necessity to involve two spheres bounded off from one another. Yet, from the side of God, such a boundary exists, and the habitual ignoring of this fact imperils the success of the Christian message, for it gives non-Christian peoples, whose experience of God, at its best and purest, is grounded on this boundary, an impression of naivete and lack of insight. That God, although he is the totality of being, deigns to become a partner of man, is the most paradoxical of marvels, one which, posited once and for all by God, never ceases to impress on our minds its character of utter incomprehensibility. For this reason, the Christian preacher must treat the religious experience of other peoples with the most profound and sincere respect—even and especially that of the Asiatics. If he fails in this, he must blame himself for his inability to convey the gospel message to them in acceptable terms.

3. Ultimately we cannot altogether dismiss a treatment of the problem which proceeds not so much on logical as on historical lines, according to the changes in man's general outlook. Every period of the Church's history has its own distinctive characteristics. There is, undeniably, a development of humanity, and even of human consciousness in general, though, to forestall any objection, we do not necessarily thereby mean "progress." Further the presence of Christianity (which does not itself develop, or at any rate not in the same sense) within humanity is, in some degree, involved in this development. Consequently we need not

143

hesitate in saying that, through the continuing presence of the Christian element, which expands and gradually leavens the whole mass, certain changes in the common consciousness of mankind may result. For example, there are certain values whose source is Christian and, therefore, whose final justification lies in Christianity, such as love for one's enemies, the recognition of the rights of one's opponents, of others precisely as such, of one's neighbors in general. These values may be taken over by all men, even non-Christians, and form an integral part of their mentality. The present epoch, just beginning, may be rightly described as one of the encounters of men with one another precisely as men, that is, quite apart from their environment in the world of nature. It is, therefore, an anthropological epoch, in contrast with the cosmological epoch of the past. What characterized the latter was that man was looked on as a part of the whole (macro-)cosmos, which itself appeared as a part, to be defined with more and more precision, of the Absolute, the divine—the spheres led up directly from the earth to God's heaven, the stars were of an imperishable substance and moved by angels, and so the cosmos was a direct revelation of the Godhead, the "unknown God" of Paul's speech on the Areopagus. Consequently the "natural knowledge of God" was attained simply and directly through the cosmos; this was true even of Hölderlin in his contemplation of the ether or the sun, and of Goethe with his nature as God.

The present time, however, is the age of technology and science, when the human mind dominates the material cosmos, which, in consequence, no longer leads the mind beyond itself to God. The natural knowledge of God, therefore, is not to be reached in the same way as before.

Nietzsche's "God is dead" was prompted by the cosmos as "emptied of God," if we ignore, for the moment, the discredited Strauss Christianity of the nineteenth century. The same phenomenon today may well be the clue to the understanding of Karl Barth's critique of the natural knowledge of God; that is, he criticizes it from the standpoint of the present state of development of the human mind. It is beyond question that Paul, in the present condition of natural science, would have spoken differently on the Areopagus. All this does not mean that, now that the cosmological epoch is over, we are also to discard the natural knowledge of God and the *analogia entis* as obsolete. But it does mean that, while the essence of natural religion remains the same, the forms it takes and the experiences on which it is based may change, and the resultant modifications have to be noted.

The situation of man as regards God is not essentially altered. The contemplatives and mystics of old experienced the unreality of the world in the presence of the Absolute; but has not the technological world of today the same, or an intensified, phantomlike unreality to the eyes of anyone who suddenly awakes from it? What, if not this, is the cause of all our neuroses and the antidotes we adopt which are no less unreal? It is in the unreality of our world that there speaks, as ever, the one, imperishable, wholly other reality, the Word. We search nowadays for formulas; but the Word is no formula. It cannot be manipulated or put to serve our purposes. It serves no interest and, therefore, seems to most people to be without interest for them. A formula is something that has found adequate verbal expression; but the Word remains always unique and inexpressible.

145

Some Points of Eschatology

1. The Present Situation

Eschatology is the storm center of the theology of our times. It is the source of severe squalls that threaten all the theological fields, and makes them fruitful, beating down or reinvigorating their various growths. Troeltsch's dictum: "The bureau of eschatology is usually closed" was true enough of the liberalism of the nineteenth century, but since the turn of the century the office has been working overtime. The whole of liberal theology was radically recast by de Wette, Weiss, Albert Schweitzer and Martin Werner in taking the "parousia that has yet to come" as the starting point, that is to say, eschatology. The counter-movement of Karl Barth and his followers is a school which expounds the whole of theology eschatologically. And though Barth himself, since his *Church Dogmatics,* has abjured an exclusive preoccupation with eschatology, yet it is a fact that his reconstruction of the whole of Protestant theology, starting from a complete rejection of the Augustinian and Calvinist doctrine of predestination, is done mainly from an eschatological standpoint. The third principal current of theological thought that produced Bultmann's demythologizing and existentializing of theology likewise has its source in eschatology, both in a negative sense, in that the structure of the "mythical" is essentially concerned with the *eschata,* and positively, since the whole of faith is reduced to the fulfillment of Christ's death and resurrection in the believer.

Nonetheless, it is easy to understand that the remolding of theology by eschatology has not brought about a settled systematic structure. On the contrary, the last things show up the confused state of the theology. There is no "system" of the last things; and, when they are taken as the point around which a system of theology is to be erected, the closed lines of the preceding dogmatic treatises are opened, and even become entangled. Emil Brunner, writing in 1953, pointed out frankly: "If we ask what this theology, my own included, . . . has achieved in the formulation of eschatology, we must admit, to our shame and astonishment, that here all we can see is a great vacuum. Hardly anything of real significance has been attained."[1] But perhaps the appearance is deceptive. It is no small achievement for a whole generation of theologians to have learned to pursue theology in the presence of an eschatology whose horizon is left open. In this way, they will gradually come to realize the character of the *eschata* as molding the whole of theological thought, and work out their theology accordingly.

Unlike Protestant theology, Catholic theology does not advance by leaping from extreme to extreme; but it cannot indefinitely forego considering the same problems, and proposing solutions of a more moderate kind. In fact, there is great activity going on here, admittedly often behind the scenes; the shutters remain up, "pending alterations." What is being done is on such a scale and goes so deep that it

[1] *Das Ewige als Zukunft und Gegenwart,* Zurich 1953, 231.

would be presumptuous in a few pages even to offer anything like a "progress report," and certainly it is out of the question to display the results, which at present are quite impossible to assess. All one can do is to indicate a few directions of theological thought and research; they are basic to Catholic thinking and may well become of more and more importance. Out of the vast mass of publications (those on eschatology alone, in its various aspects, are considerable) only a few works can be cited: those which seem to bring out clearly the main lines.[1]

The literature in question can be divided into four classes, in which the various topics merge into one another:

1. That which deals with the subject as if nothing of moment had occurred in the past fifty years, or as if it could all be incorporated into the old framework of the medieval and Counter-reformation treatises by a few additional observations. For the most part, this literature consists of textbooks for students, either recast anew or readaptations of the old.

2. A number of works of *haute vulgarisation,* in which distinguished authors propose, in essay form, a summary or general account of the whole problem of eschatology or an important part, with a view to contributing to an improvement in the general treatment.[2]

3. The most significant work is that devoted to specialized subjects. It poses new questions in all fields of eschatology, makes us see old ones in a new way, or else brings up ones

[1] The copious literature of the last decades can be found mentioned in the works of M. Schmaus, *Von den letzten Dingen,* Munster 1948, and volume 4 of *Kirchliche Dogmatik,* Munich 1953, 254ff.

[2] For example, Alois Winklhofer's *The Coming of His Kingdom,* New York 1963.

that have been forgotten, and teaches us to see the statements of scripture and tradition in a more revealing light. As long as these specialized studies are pursued in a living spirit, their conclusions scrupulously tested, their proposals securely based, we can reconcile ourselves to, even rejoice in the fact that new stones have not been incorporated into an already existing structure.

4. A comprehensive account of present-day eschatology hardly exists. On the Protestant side, *Die Letzten Dinge* (frequently re-edited and recast) may be considered as such, though it has been the subject of much dispute, and has many serious defects. There is nothing similar on the Catholic side, for the best claimant; *Von den letzten Dingen* (1948) by Schmaus, despite its more than seven hundred pages, is more of a collection, excellent indeed, of the different standpoints and their development than a speculative treatment and critique. So far there has been no representative monograph written from the Catholic standpoint, such as those resulting from the vigorous Protestant discussions on eschatology, Cullmann's *Christ and Time*, for example, and the works of the Swedish school. We shall, therefore, attend chiefly to the works in the third category, so as to gain a few indications—all that can be expected—of the direction of present-day studies.

We may conclude this introductory section by emphasizing, though it should not really be necessary, that all the inquiries now in progress do nothing to shake or cast doubt on the established doctrines of the Church. We refer to such doctrines as the universality of death as the consequence of sin; the cessation, with death, of the time of merit; the particular judgment; the immediate entrance of the soul on the beatific vision after expiating venial sin or the discharge

150

of temporal punishment in purgatory, or else its entrance on the state of eternal damnation in hell; the Lord's parousia at the end of time; the bodily resurrection of all for the last judgment. Those parts of eschatology that belong to the defined content of faith can be found in any standard theological work; they are not the concern of the present essay. There is, however, another range of questions concerning what lies beyond the bounds of the world of space and time, what happens to man at death, the dissolution of the world into its elements, the passing away of heaven and earth, the termination of history and the gathering of its fruits into the barns of eternity, the judgment on creation and its final state in God. All such matters, it will be readily understood, need to be constantly examined afresh, in case any sense-images, scientific or other hypotheses creep in unobserved which, though they may help to elucidate a part of the truth, soon reveal themselves as merely provisional. We may say that the present studies make no attempt to further the exposition of the message of revelation in its fullness, as is clear from the simplifications which, as we shall see, may be considered the basic feature of modern eschatological thought. It may well be a mission reserved to a subsequent generation to develop from the core of truth now disclosed a more extensive and adequate body of speculation.

2. The Reduction

Theologians were aware, even before Bultmann's time, that the modern picture of the world, as regards both the structure of nature and its "history," is quite other than the anthropomorphic cosmology of the ancient world, including

151

Israel, and that it devolved on them, however hazardous the enterprise, to prize out revealed truth from the ancient framework of ideas and insert it into the modern. In a sense, there must be a repetition of the experience which Origen passed through when he was faced with the contrast between the few thousand years of biblical history and the gnostic idea of the abysses of time known as "aeons," and solved the problem thus posed in favor of the faith by taking his stand squarely on a christocentric (in the guise of a logocentric) position. In the nineteenth century men's minds were staggered by the discovery of the enormous span of human history between "Adam" and Abraham. The "aeons" from the beginning of the world to Adam are far more baffling to the imagination. These factors, together with the intimation we now have of the true dimensions of the cosmos, in fact of its continual expansion, seemed at first to make the biblical "end of the world" completely irrelevant to the world we knew. Not only must we discard, therefore, any localization of the eschatological "places" (heaven, hell, purgatory, limbo) in the one world—since that means their transference from a theological cosmos, whose higher and lower regions are the divine and demonic, to a physical—but also cease to regard any "end of time" (say, of the planet earth) as an event relevant to theology. In consequence, the last things of man, of his history and of the cosmos, must be carried over into an entirely new dimension, which strictly belongs only to revelation and faith. This, in turn, has two consequences. The first is that these *eschata* become, in another way, inaccessible to thought, since the whole system of the world, the whole man in his course from birth to death, is taken up into a single dimension manifested by God's revelation of his dealings with the world. The second is that theology as a whole must be dominated by the *eschata,* become "eschatologized," for now the world, the man, and history realize their true nature only when subjected to God's transforming action.

In other words, the so-called last things, merely because they have become inaccessible to thought, are all the more actual. They have become the "last events" affecting the being and the history of man and the world.[1] It is no longer the "last things" that are incorporated into a cosmos understood in the ancient theological sense; it is the cosmos which is now carried over beyond itself into the action of God. This, certainly, involves the danger of a certain "acosmism,"[2] the assertion of a direct relation of the creature with the *"Deus nudus,"* who becomes its "last end," in place of all the "things" and "states." But does this not bring us back precisely to the main theme of revelation? Long before Bultmann, Père Lagrange, the great exegete, observed, in connection with one of the most wonderful passages on hope in the Old Testament, (the end of psalm 72: "I am always with thee . . . For what have I in heaven, and besides thee

[1] "Eschatology is becoming, in theological thought, once more what it is in scripture and the fathers, namely the true significance of history, a significance which, elucidating the whole mystery of the Church, acts as a ferment in the present order of things, and this order will only be understood fully in its final outcome. This sense for the eschatological element is what has most been lacking to ecclesiology since the sixteenth century. Without it, men looked on the last things not so much as the end and fulfillment of the entire order of creation as an accumulation of 'things,' somehow present behind the curtain of death, and which could be studied like the 'things' of earth. They asked: *Quid sit ignis purgatorius? Utrum visio Dei sit per speciem?* just as they inquired, in physics, into the nature of fire, or in epistemology into knowledge through a species. In short, they went in for a kind of physics of the last things. Most of our textbooks on eschatology hark back to this type." Y. Congar in *Rev.Sc.Ph.Th.,* 1949, 463.

[2] As may be seen in the "consequent eschatologism" of the young Barth in *Epistle to the Romans* (1922).

153

what do I desire upon earth? . . . But it is good for me to adhere to my God"): "This is no sort of description of hell or paradise: God alone remains before the psalmist's gaze, and he desires only God. To be with God—in heaven or on earth: that is enough. Nothing about cosmology! Here we stand at the center of Israel's faith."[1] But we must not forget that for the great theologians, just as for scripture, everything in the way of cosmology was merely an accompaniment to the main theme: *Ipse (Deus) post istam vitam sit locus noster* (Augustine).[2] God is the "last thing" of the creature. Gained, he is heaven; lost, he is hell; examining, he is judgment; purifying, he is purgatory. He it is to whom finite being dies, and through whom it rises to him, in him. This he is, however, as he presents himself to the world, that is, in his Son, *Jesus Christ,* who is the revelation of God and, therefore, the whole essence of the last things.[3] In this way, eschatology is, almost more even than any other *locus theologicus,* entirely a doctrine of *salvation.* This is, as we shall see, absolutely central.

This enables us to understand why present eschatological thought is so pronouncedly antiplatonist, often to the point of animosity. The "philosophic solution" of the problem of how man and the world could be eternal despite death and time was at best (after the recourse to magic in the East,

[1] *Revue Biblique,* 1905, 195f.

[2] En. in ps. 30, n.8 (*PL* 36, 252) in ps. 70 n.5 (878).

[3] Jean Daniélou expresses this point well in his *Christologie et Eschatologie,* "Chalcedon," vol. 3, 269–286. He shows that the seemingly unhistorical formula of Chalcedon really contains a biblical and patristic theology of history, and, as it were, takes it for granted. According to this viewpoint, Christ in the hypostatic union of the two natures is the *Eschaton* which governs the time both of the promise and of the fulfillment, and essentially, as he who has come, is the one coming and the one who fulfills all things.

and at the time of the pantheistic solutions put forward by the Stoa) the Socratic and Platonist one of distinguishing in man a mortal part (the body) and an immortal one (the soul). Accordingly the word "immortal" presupposes that only the body dies, not the man. Thus the mortal part, in dying, separates from the immortal, though this view fails to take account of the principal element in the phenomenon of death. The whole difficulty for thought—so greatly increased by the very terms of the gospel of salvation—of securing the salvation of the whole man with God was assumed by the psalmist and the prophets; and the necessity, inaccessible to the human view, of this salvation with God must logically, though equally inaccessible to the mind (since it is impossible to justify philosophically), be worked out from the New Testament hope of resurrection for man and the world.[1]

It is just *because* the event wherein the cosmos enters on the "last end" is not capable of explanation in cosmological, intra-historical terms that God's final act of redemption must be an act done *on* the creature, a new forming of the creature *itself*. The "otherness" of the New Aeon is a making other, a making new, of the Old; it is not a matter of throw-

[1] Platonism clearly dominated western, even Christian, thinking down to the threshold of modern times; we have only to think of the stress laid on the "immortality of the soul," and how the resurrection was held to be an almost unnecessary "accidental blessedness" superadded to the substantial blessedness already possessed (Denz. 530). And, despite all the counter-arguments of philosophers, such as those of the Stoics and the later Greek philosophers in general, the ancient cosmos remained always something in the nature of a "house," a body (*magnum corpus*) of souls. Greek and medieval man never really thought acosmically. The crisis of Platonism only came with the change in man's image of the world. With this, two things became necessary: the express rejection of the relationship of the souls of the dead to the world, and the equally express incorporation of them into the glorified humanity of Christ.

155

ing over the created world and making another, quite different one in its place. Bultmann's concern to apply all revealed truth existentially to man and his world is to be thoroughly approved. But the actual event of this change from the Old to the New Aeon is the same as Christ's transition from death to resurrection: his "return" to the Father is the *creation of the dimension* into which, by the free grace of God, man and the cosmos begin to be transformed: "heaven's real becoming."[1] The death of the believer (and, through him, of man generally) is the "incorporation" of the soul into the heavenly body, heavenly "temple," heavenly "house" of the risen humanity of Christ. This is true whether, following the preponderant theological tradition, we make the resurrection of the dead commence in the middle of history with Christ's resurrection (see Mt 27:52; and not alone Mary in her bodily assumption, as the "accompaniment" to his ascension required by the social character of Christ's bodily condition),[2] or whether we follow M. Feuillet in taking the "house not made with hands, eternal in heaven" of 2 Cor 5:1 to mean Christ's transfigured humanity, and so the "intermediate state" of which Paul speaks not as a "purely spiritual" one.[3] The resurrection of Christ and, with it, eschatology take now a far more pronouncedly central place

[1] K. Rahner, "The Resurrection of the Body," *Theological Investigations,* vol. 2, 203ff.

[2] H. Zeller, "Corpora Sanctorum, a Study of Mt 27:52–53," *ZKathTh* 71, 1949, 385–465.

[3] *Destinée des chrétiens et fondements de l'eschatologie paulienne:* "La demeure céleste est le corps glorieux du Christ, mais a titre de prèmices de la nouvelle création, c'est à dire, en tant q'incluant virtuellement le corps glorieux de tous les chrétiens." "L'incorporation au Christ constitue le fondement de l'eschatologie paulinienne." See M. Feuillet, "La demeure céleste et la destinée des chrétiens," *Rech. SC. Rel.,* 1956, 161–192, 360–402.

in Catholic theology than previously. F. X. Durwell,[1] without the least allusion to Barth[2] or Bultmann, has rearranged the whole of theology around this center, and made the Church, the sacraments, the Eucharist, even justification and the whole Christian life proceed from it.

Before we go on to see how the *eschaton* of Christ, as God's dealing with man, determines, absolutely speaking, the final condition of man and the world, we must explain what happened to Christ in such a way that the last things are elucidated as aspects of an event which is christological and ecclesiological in character.

It needs only a renewed attention to a fundamental theme of the theology of the first centuries[3] to realize that, despite historical interpretations[4] and attempts at demythologizing[5] and at showing the idea to be unscriptural,[6] the descent into hell between Christ's death and resurrection is a necessary expression of the event of the redemption—not, indeed (as on Good Friday), within the history actually in progress, but (on Holy Saturday) in the history already accomplished of the old aeon, in the sheol of the Old Testament. Here it is important to remember that, contrary to all the escha-

---

[1] *The Resurrection,* New York 1960.

[2] In my book on Karl Barth I have shown that this "consequent christocentricism" can be developed in a genuinely Catholic sense, and that the leading Catholic theologians of today think, for the greater part, along these lines.

[3] A. Grillmeier, "Der Gottessohn im Totenreich. Die Descensuslehre in der älteren christlichen Uberlieferung," *ZKathTh* 71, 1949, 1–53, 184–204.

[4] See the great work, not yet fully utilized, of J. Kroll, *Gott und Hölle. Der Mythus vom Descensuskampfe,* Berlin 1932.

[5] For instance, in the historical *aperçus* of Rivière on the doctrine of satisfaction.

[6] W. Bieder, *Die Vorstellung von der Höllenfahrt Jesu Christi,* Zurich 1949.

tological ideas of later, moralistic Judaism,[1] in the "beyond"
there was no entrance into heaven (Heb 11:39–40) "before" (logically speaking) Christ's death and descent into
sheol. Fundamentally the goods of salvation (such as faith,
hope, charity) in sheol—assuming there to be such—must
be considered, at best, a kind of "anticipation" of the illumination brought by the redeemer's descent into that "temporal
poena damni" (Pohle-Gierens, Dogm. III, 660). It must be
emphasized that the believer also understands what damnation really is—taking the term strictly theologically and in
its primary sense—when he takes full account of the *termi-
nus a quo* of the redemption. The darkness into which sinful
humanity must sink becomes evident at the moment when—
in Christ's "descent" into (we do not say the "place," but)
the "state" of perdition[2]—this darkness becomes a yawning
abyss ready to be illuminated by the light of the redemption. The mystery of Holy Saturday is two things simul-
taneously: the utmost extremity of the *exinanitio* and the
beginning of the *gloria* even before the resurrection. This
was the view of the fathers, as it is today the idea of redemption in the Eastern Church. Only with Christ's descent
into the stagnation of sheol does there come into being, in
the "beyond," something in the nature of a "way," a mode
of access; and this means that "purgatory," meaning the

[1] Which, of course, possessed a subtly nuanced doctrine of the Beyond
(see P. Volz: *Die Eschatologie der Jüdischen Gemeinden im neutesta-
mentlichen Zeitalter nach den Quellen der rabbinischen, apokalyptischen
und apokryphen Literatur dargestellt*, Tübingen 1934). But Plato possessed one also.

[2] Of course, this does not mean approval of Calvin's doctrine, for
the reason that the continuous *visio immediata Dei in anima Christi*
makes his experience of hell wholly incommensurate with any other,
gives it an "exemplary," soteriological and trinitarian significance.

158

aspect of the judgment that opens to the sinner a purifying passage through fire, had no existence in the Old Testament (either in the logical or temporal order), and could only be *created* through the "evacuation" of sheol. In this respect, Thomas' doctrine that the fire of hell and that of purgatory are the same fire (IV, 21, 1) contains a certain truth, though, on the other hand, it is precisely this part of medieval theology with its main stress on the localized *receptacula* that most needs revision.[1]

The reduction of "purgatory" from a "place" to a "state" means little enough unless one is also prepared to ascribe the purifying character of this state to the encounter of the as yet unpurified sinner with the Kyrios appearing to him in judgment. Certainly we may agree with Joachim Gnilka who, after reviewing the whole range of exegesis and referring the "testing fire" of the day of the Lord to Christ's coming at the last judgment, then represents this fire (in view of Is 66:15–16) simply as an "image of the majesty of God revealing himself . . . the inapproachability of the

---

[1] M. Jugie, unfortunately, expresses the situation correctly, when he says (perhaps with a certain deliberate humor): "*Saint-Thomas . . . soutient que cette visite du Sauveur aux séjours d'outre-tombe ne changea rien au cours normal de la justice divine pour ce qui regarde le purgatoire,*" *Le Purgatoire et les moyens de l'éviter,* Paris. And the same may be said of the third and fourth *receptacula,* limbo and hell. And since in the "forehell" supernatural hope must be considered present, nothing at all really happens (in the sense of the redemptive *happening*). What a departure from early Christianity! A purely static, because cosmological, eschatology was not capable of representing the *event* of Christ's passage through the state of perdition. The extreme example of this inability is one not even to be tolerated theologically as poetic license: Dante's representation of a Christian's "passage" (on the steps of Christ or only of the pagan Virgil?) through hell, in which nothing happens of relevance to salvation.

All-holy."[1] On the other hand, it is undeniable that, according to the Bible, there are not two judgments or judgment days, but only one, and, therefore, we must see the particular judgment after death in some kind of dynamic connection with the last judgment. It would, moreover, be a great gain for the ecumenical dialogue if we could understand the so-called "purgatorial fire" as a dimension of judgment, as the sinner's encounter with Christ's "eyes as a flame of fire" and "feet . . . as a burning furnace" (Ap 1:14 = Dn 10:6). Y. Congar, in his important study on purgatory,[2] points out that the Church has made very few factual pronouncements on it, and that it is to be interpreted soteriologically in connection with the *Descensus* (here of the mystical body).[3] If this idea of encounter is applied consistently, then the judgment too will be interpreted in full accord with the Bible as the sinner coming face to face with the redeemer as judge.[4] The indissoluble unity of judgment and redemption, justice and mercy on the cross is the warrant for the rightness of the New Testament demand on Christians to await the judgment as the presentation (parousia) of the truth of the cross and resurrection in an attitude of both fear and hope, and to persevere therein, watching and praying for the Lord's coming, this being the absolutely basic Christian attitude. This existential New

[1] Gnilka, 126: "Christus autem est ut ignis purissimus, qui est inseparabilis a luce, . . . et est ignis ille spiritualis vitae et intellectus, qui ut omnia consumens, intra se receptans, omnia et probat et judicat quasi judicium materialis ignis, cuncta examinans . . . Ita Christus judex secundum unicum simplicissimum atque indistinctum judicium in une momento . . ." Nicholas of Cusa, *De Docta Ignorantia*, III, 9.

[2] In *Le mystère de la mort et sa célebration*, Paris 1951.

[3] *Ibid.*, 284.

[4] See D. Mollat, art. *Judgment*. Dict. Bibl. Suppl.

Testament doctrine on the last things has nothing to do with the idea of a proximate coming, and is not to be made conditional on it. It is more in the nature of the final attitude and act of the Christian, the final state of his knowledge in faith, which is not strengthened but weakened, not deepened but made more superficial, if the believer presumes any knowledge of the outcome of the judgment, rather than persevering in hope and fear, action and endurance.

Once theologians (doubtless *bona fide* and thinking that faith demands it) consider they have "certainty of faith"[1] about the outcome of the judgment, they decide in advance, unknowingly, a whole range of questions, and the consequences necessarily reach into what would seem the most remote parts of theology. These unavoidable conclusions, however, are clearly inconsistent with what the Bible teaches on salvation, and so reveal their questionable nature. The claim to know the outcome of the judgment (in the sense of certain knowledge that the judge will condemn some) has, at least, three consequences. They were all, as a matter of logic, received into theology, once eschatology had taken on this basic pattern, that is to say at the time of Augustine. First, despite the consistently positively conceived idea of predestination in scripture, which left the matter open, men were obliged to adopt a doctrine of double predestination, equally oppressive whether *ante* or *post praevisa merita*. Christian belief thus took on that dark and menacing aspect

---

[1] For example, Fulgentinus, *De fide*, rule 35: "Hold with firm, unshakeable faith that not only all pagans, but also all Jews, heretics and schismatics who terminate their lives outside the Catholic Church, will go into everlasting fire, prepared for the devil and his angels" (*PL* 65,704). What is significant is not so much the extreme character of the statement itself as the fact that knowledge of the (this!) outcome of judgment should be put forward as an article of faith.

161

which brought untold suffering to mankind in the middle
ages and the Reformation, even to the men of the Counter-
reformation. It was a spirit in strong contrast with that of
early Christianity and the patristic era. We are just now
beginning, in conformity with scripture, to grope our way
by degrees to a more objective position. Secondly, when
Christ is not looked on as the *Eschaton,* but when the results
of the judgment are considered as "objects" capable of being known, the character of faith undergoes a change. Instead of a loving and trusting submission of the whole person
to the personal divine truth of the Father in the Son, it becomes, of necessity, an intellectual, neutral act embracing in-
differently truths both of salvation and reprobation and,
therefore, only when it is directed to a truth of salvation can
it comprise love and hope and trust.[1] With this is closely
connected a strangely truncated idea of hope, since it now
seems against faith to hope for the salvation of all men;
though this clearly conflicts with the biblical idea of hope.
Furthermore it means that Christ cannot have prayed for
the *reprobi,* since his prayer cannot fail.[2] Thirdly, this de-
ciding in advance entails attributing to a most important
series of scriptural texts, which make the salvation of all

[1] "On the other hand, one can yet believe what one does not hope
for. What believer does not believe, for example, in the punishments
of the godless? But he will not hope for it. . . . Faith, therefore, is related to both good and evil, since one may believe in both good and
evil, and with good, not with evil faith." Augustine, *Enchiridion,* c. 8.
And so right up to the high middle ages.

[2] Thomas, III, 22, 4, ad 2: *Dominus mon oravit pro omnibus crici-
fixoribus neque etiam pro omnibus qui erant credituri in eum, sed pro
his solum qui erant praedestinati, ut per ipsum vitam consequerentur
aeternam.* If this were the case, the prayer of the Church, according
to 1 Tim 2:1f., would have a wider scope than Christ's, which, however,
in Jn 17, seems absolutely universal (v. 2 and notwithstanding v. 12).

162

something to be hoped for (though unknowable), a sense which takes away part of the force they clearly possess.

Human thought always has the urge to "systematize"; but scripture lets the possible, indeed the actual twofold outcome of the judgment remain "unreconciled" alongside the prospect of universal reconciliation; nor is there any possibility of subordinating one to the other. Origen attempted this from one standpoint, reducing hell to a kind of purgatory, and so weakening what scripture says of the judgment. Augustine (and the theologians who followed him) did so from the opposite standpoint, depriving the hope of universal redemption of all foundation. Yet this too enfeebles faith in eschatological doctrine, as was well understood by Charles Péguy who, on account of the "intolerableness" of what was taught about hell, left the Church, returning to it when he found a kind of "solution." This he expressed in his "Mystère de Jeanne d'Arc," where Joan, with her inward "revolt" against the possible damnation of her brothers, the sinners, suddenly realizes in prayer that she is at one with God himself in her revolt against the loss of anyone at all. As regards scripture, Christ's statements about the judgment (particularly Mt 25:31f.) are not intended to impart a placid "knowledge" of facts, unfortunately unalterable, which like the damnation of a part of mankind must be accepted with resignation. Concerning the *"effort incroyable, terrible de volonté d'humilité"* of Madame Gervaise,[1] Joan perceives behind the appearance that *"au fond elle en prend son parti. Elle en souffre beaucoup, mais au fond, tout au fond, elle en prend son parti . . . Elles s'y*

[1] Péguy, *Oeuvres poétiques compl.* Paris, 151.

résignent. Elles s'y habituent. Mais vous, mon Dieu, vous ne vous n'y habituez pas. Vos saints ne s'y habituent pas. Jésus, votre Saint, ne s'y habitue pas. Vous ne vous y résignez pas . . . Mon Dieu, j'ai des prières secrètes. Vous le savez. Je vous suis confidente."[1]

Of course, from the standpoint of theology, there are important reservations to be made as regards this poetical passage. No one, not even the saint, can simply equate his earthly wishes and hopes with the "hope" of God and of Christ, without that absolute Christian *indifference* to the two, which is necessary even, and particularly, as regards the judgment passed, but is not the same as a purely passive "acceptance." There is, however, one thing that can be said of Péguy's adoption of an eschatology that leaves open the outcome of the judgment that is bound up with the person of the redeemer and judge, and renounces any final systematization: it is that this has always been characteristic of the eschatology of the mystics, for whom the experiences of the "dark night" and of "hell" always had a soteriological meaning (we may instance the two Matildas, Gertrude, Bridget, Teresa, John of the Cross, also Eckhart, Nicholas of Cusa, and so many others who had some experience of the divine darkness). Péguy, as well as Claudel[2] and Bernanos, thinks along the same lines of Teresa of Lisieux with her absolute hope,[3] in whose wake follows the whole "theology of hope," with its practical orientation, as developed over the last decade in France and now developing

[1] *Ibid.*, 1347.
[2] For example, the *Cantique de Palmyre* (in *Conversations dans le Loire et Cher*).
[3] See my *Therese of Lisieux*, New York.

164

in Germany.[1] This line of thought, however, will only remain within the obedience of faith if it avoids the opposite pitfall of an esoteric Origenism with its opposition to the eschatology of the Church and her preaching on the grounds of its being antiquated.[2] If the "reduction" here developed is accepted, one cannot, at the same time, attempt a contrary (secretly gnostic) systematization. Gottlieb Söhngen put the matter well, in Kantian terminology, when he said that the redemption of the entire creation might well be a *regulative idea,* but could never be a *constitutive principle* of theology.

The process of reduction must also be applied to the theology of the *Limbus puerorum.* This question has lately been raised anew by, among others, Peter Gumpel S.J.[3] The

[1] Gabriel Marcel, *Homo Viator,* New York.

[2] "No one can assert with real authority that there is no hell any longer, but it will, nonetheless, no longer be taken into calculation" (*Wort und Wahrheit* 11, May 1956, 330). Consequently the present "theology of hell" needs, at times, to be handled with great care (one good account, though only provisional, is the joint work of Bardy, Carrouges, Dorival, Spicq, Heres and Guitton: *L'enfer,* ed. Rev. des Jeunes, Paris 1950; the collected essays, *Satan,* of the *Études Carmelitaines* 1948, are open to serious objections). The fact that so many theologians avoid the subject only shows that they are aware of its difficulty. Anyone who approaches it today must be conversant with biblical theology as well as historical and systematic theology. In fact, he must have made up his mind on a "theological gnoseology of the eschatological statements considered in their possibility and their limits," and also whether "these limits are the same for 'heaven' and for 'hell,' or whether (what would be more correct) we are bound in certain respects to deny this. This would then have to be kept in mind when in what follows the two final states are treated of in succession as though they were on the same level" (Karl Rahner, *Theological Investigations,* vol. 1, Baltimore 1961, 36).

[3] "Unbaptized Infants, May They Be Saved?" *Downside Review* 1954, 342–458, with comprehensive list of works. "Unbaptized Infants, a Further Report" (*ibid.,* 1955, 317–346), in which additional writers are cited and answered.

limits of eschatological thought during this life's pilgrimage are made very clear here. Finally, as Karl Rahner has repeatedly pointed out, the connection between the *visio beatifica*, between "heaven" and the risen humanity of Christ, has been almost entirely neglected by theologians.

We may conclude with one observation. The *eschata* must be interpreted throughout christologically, which means, at the deepest level, in trinitarian terms. This applies to the judgment, purgatory, hell and sheol (which, in its biblical sense, is by no means the innocuous "forehell" it has been made into). Only then will eschatology be sufficiently decosmologized, freed of the remnants of sub-Christian philosophy, and become, in its object, an integral part of personal obedience in faith to Jesus Christ.

3. EXPANSION

The results that follow from an eschatology based on christological principles extend to every sphere of theology and, beyond that, to a philosophical interpretation of man and the world in the light of revelation. They are, in fact, so extensive and involved that we cannot give here even a cursory glance at them. All that is possible is a rapid and approximate enumeration of the questions that arise and that concern the present time. They are, first, questions within eschatology itself; second, those about the effects of eschatology on the rest of theology; third, those concerning the encounter between theology and philosophy in view of a convergence of the natural and supernatural finality of man and the cosmos, or of an integration of the factors, known to us, of natural eschatology into the more comprehensive data of the Christian faith. These three, however, are constantly overlapping; and, if we wish to keep abreast of the progress made in this field, we must always keep all three together in mind.

1. Today we can only build up eschatology by taking account of the structure of theology in general, and, in addition, of our present understanding of the world and of man. In every epoch, the Church comes to look on the Old and New Testaments in a fresh light, gaining understanding for the value of a particular text in the light of its historical setting, its context in religious history and in the history of revelation. The insights thus gained may lead her to propose criticism (often far-reaching) of the traditional exegesis; but as a result of some slight transpositions, they may also bring to light new and valid aspects of traditional thought.

There is no question of "demythologization," which, as the results show, splits asunder the body and soul of revelation, and ends up in an arid existentialism, narrow and unconvincing. It is, instead, a matter of explaining the word of God in the text it has assumed. For instance, concerning the Old Testament idea of sheol, we can adduce parallels from the Near East, show that Platonism represents a higher stage of thought in religious history, prove that Judaism at the time of Christ possessed a far more detailed eschatology than that of the great prophets and psalmists. Nonetheless this apparently "imperfect" doctrine is the most decisive for theology; it is the point of access to the redemptive act of Christ which we must not simply circumvent, which, in many ways, the subtler Greek eschatology fails to elucidate. Even the concrete representations of sheol with

167

their anthropomorphic characteristics are not to be discarded, but interpreted theologically. This is the only way to achieve, by degrees, a fully developed eschatology. The same considerations apply throughout to the expectation of the Messiah.[1] They are valid, too, for the study of the differences in the ideas of time within the Old Testament itself, as also for the differences between the Old and New Testaments. In this connection, new light may be thrown on the whole complex of ideas, already known to the fathers, concerning the distinction between time of promise and time of fulfillment, in fact between the three times of mere promise (the Old Testament), of fulfilled promise along with fulfillment promised (the Church of the New Testament), and complete fulfillment (eschatology). Dodd's "realized eschatology" and, opposed to it, Cullmann's "preparatory [*vorlaufende*] time" help, by their mutual dialectic, toward an understanding of the biblical idea of time.[2] For the latter overlaps the ideas of time held by various peoples and by philosophers, which ideas revelation both judges and adjusts itself to.[3] In consequence, the situation, in its historical aspect, shows itself more complicated than was foreseen. The "revealed religion" of Iran seems to agree with Judaism and Christianity in holding to an historical time striving to an end instead of to a cyclical

[1] See *L'attente du Messie*, by Cerfaux, Coppens, de Langhe and others, Desclee 1954, with copious references by W. G. Kümmel, "Verheissung und Erfüllung," Untersuchung zur eschatologischen Verkündigung Jesu. *Abh. z. Theol. d. u. N.T.* 6, Zurich 1945.

[2] See E. C. Rust, "Time and Eternity in Biblical Thought," *Theology Today*, Princeton 1953, 327–356.

[3] We may select, out of the deluge of works comparing the biblical with the Greek conception of time, J. Guitton's *Le temps et l'éternité chez Platon et St. Augustin*, Paris 1933.

time of nature. Once again, as in the case of the idea of the "resurrection"[1] and "individual eschatology" (as in "particular judgment" and "immortality"),[2] we come upon data of a *preparatio evangelica* whose theological bearing has not been sufficiently investigated.

Still more comprehensive is the work to be done on the actual eschatological texts of scripture, those of the prophets and the apocalyptic parts, in which Christ and his apostles adopt the modes of expression of the current apocalyptic, but only to bring out the full meaning of the prophetic vision and to complete it.[3] It is not a question of reviving a past form, but of inserting the central revelation of the fullness of time into the form prepared by the prophetic writings. This form is what Martin Buber describes as that of the *"Alternativik,"*[4] and it is, of its nature, repugnant to any systematization, since it is "dialogical." From this firm standpoint the interpretation of the apocalyptic form becomes exceptionally difficult; discussion on it is in progress,

[1] F. Nötscher, *Altorientalischer und alttestamentlicher Auferstehungsglaube,* Würzburg 1926.

[2] J. Bonsirven, *Le Judaisme palestinien au temps de Jésus Christ,* Paris 1934; J.-B. Frey, "La vie de l'au-delà dans les conceptions juives au temps de Jésus Christ," *Bibl.* 13, 1932, 129–168; Y. Trémel, "L'homme entre la mort et la résurrection d'après le Nouveau Testament," *L'immortalité de l'âme. Lumière et Vie* 24, 1955, 729–754.

[3] This explains the remarkable absence of a doctrine of an "intermediate state" in the New Testament, though it was worked out in contemporary Judaism (see Volz, *op. cit.*).

[4] *Der Glaube der Propheten,* Zurich 1950. "The alternative that lies in the background (of the prophetic statements about damnation) is not expressed in them (namely: "unless you be converted"). Only in this way can the word touch the depths of the soul, and perhaps stir it to the extreme act, that of conversion" (150). Admittedly, the *alternativik* can also be superseded by the statement couched quite simply in absolute terms (as in the Second Isaiah) (299).

and it will take a long time before definite clarification is reached. Questions of theological gnoseology play an important part here, among others that of the theological meaning of Christian "mysticism" (taken in the sense of Paul and John as charismatic, as opposed to the psychological and ontological tradition of modern mystical theology); only in this way can a bridge be built between biblical and ecclesiastical mysticism.[1] Mysticism is seen to have an eschatological function in the Church, and Schweitzer is not illogical when he defends both the radical eschatology of the gospel and, at the same time, the mysticism of Paul.[2] The pure apocalyptic teaching of the Bible cannot be attained merely by a consideration of "literary forms."

There is ample scope for discussion on the relations between the ancient Jewish and the Hellenic elements in the eschatology of Paul and on the projection of Alexandrian forms of thought into those of the epistle to the Hebrews. The whole history, too, of eschatological ideas in the patristic age and in later theology needs investigation. It is a vast, unexplored region which, if cultivated intelligently, should prove one of the most fruitful in the history of theology. Certainly the task can be undertaken only when biblical eschatology has achieved, to some degree, the clear outlines that can serve as normative for later theology.[3]

[1] See my book, *Thomas und die Charismatik*, Thomas-Ausgabe, vol. 23, 1954, 251–464.

[2] Emil Brunner's alternative between mysticism and word is, biblically, quite unacceptable (*Die Mystik und das Wort*, 1924), as also that of Heiler between prophetical and mystical prayer (*Das Gebet*, 1918).

[3] What Karl Rahner says in general of monographs on the history of dogma is particularly applicable to eschatology: "The greater part of these works is wholly retrospective. They do not derive from the past any impulse for the future of dogmatic theology. They show how what is

2. The work of bringing out how the *eschata* are present in all the other tracts of theology has only begun. We mention here only a few themes: the confrontation of protology (predestination, the doctrine of creation, that of paradise) with eschatology, of the history of salvation with eschatology, the Church as the presence and as the future of the last things, the relationship of sacramental doctrine and eschatology.[1] A few quite disparate materials for a theology of history have begun to be assembled. Schmaus has the merit of bringing the theology of history and apocalyptic theology back within the broad stream of eschatology, and so to have imparted to the theological treatise a fullness and concreteness it has long lacked. In addition, he has seen the necessity of remolding the whole of theology in view of the *eschata,* without on that account falling into a one-sided eschatologism ("Das Eschatologische im Christentum," *Aus der Theologie der Zeit* I, 1948, 56–84). The mystery of advent in regard to history has often been treated of by Jean Daniélou (*Essai sur le mystère de l'histoire,* Paris 1952; *Le mystère de l'Avent,* Paris 1948; *Sacramentum futuri,* Paris 1950) in answer to modern Protestant theology, and, at

accepted has come about" (*Theological Investigations,* vol. 1, 7). And the eschatology of Thomas, in his *Commentary on the Sentences,* an exhaustive treatment for the time it was written, has never been worked out fully and systematically and from an historical point of view.

[1] A few initial studies are all we have for the baptismal doctrine of Rom 6 (see Dom O. Rousseau, "La descente aux enfers, fondement sotériologique du baptême chrétien," *R. S. R. Mélanges Lebreton* II, Paris 1952, 273–297), and for the Eucharist as an eschatological meal (see Daniélou, *Mystère de l'histoire,* 211f). But there is nothing on the connection between the sacrament of penance and the resurrection, confirmation and the eschatological giving of the Spirit ("in the last days," Acts 2:17), on the relationship between the sacrament of orders and the last things. Karl Rahner has in view a new conception of the doctrine of extreme unction in connection with a theology of death.

the same time, reconstructing the patristic theology of history.

3. Finally there is the new encounter of theological and philosophical eschatology, fertile in results for both, but more fraught with difficulty than ever. Through the clear demarcation of what belongs to theology, the way is freed for new problems of philosophy to be considered, which again react fruitfully on theology. The philosophy of time and history, of man and his (natural) end, of death, of the finality of the cosmos as a whole, are today so many open fields of research that await cultivation.

The risen Christ is the fulfillment of the meaning, as prescribed by the Father, of man, history and the cosmos;[1] and, therefore, the advance of the created world cannot be indifferent or foreign to this end. All that impels the cosmos toward the realization of its meaning, while remaining subject to supernatural causality, must be integrated into the miracle of the supernatural order, of grace and redemption, the miracle of the resurrection of the body.[2] In this connection, we cannot neglect the broad stream of cosmological thought, which, continuing the high-scholastic and idealist-romantic philosophy of nature (Baader, Görres), tends now in a clearly antiplatonist and antispiritualist direction, to a rehabilitation of the body,[3] of matter,[4] of the idea of the

[1] Fr. Meister, *Die Vollendung der Welt im Opfer des Gottmenschen,* Freiburg 1938.

[2] Which, for scholasticism, is always general. See S. Th. Suppl. 75, 3: *Utrum resurrectio sit naturalis,* where the answer is a distinction: *simpliciter loquendo est miraculosa, non naturalis, nisi secundum quid.*

[3] V. Poucel S. J., *Mystique de la terre;* vol. 1, "Plaidoyer le pour corps." Preface by Paul Claudel; vol. 2, "La parabole du monde," Paris 1937, 1939. "La sensation du divine," *Présence et prophétie,* 1942.

[4] Gustav Siewerth, *Der Mensch und sein Leib,* Einsiedeln 1953. *Wort und Bild,* Schwann 1952. *Die Sinne und das Wort,* Schwann 1956.

incarnation of the spirit,[1] of sense-activity as attaining even a religious knowledge of God.[2] Hengstenberg, in a number of works,[3] has endeavored to show how these various conceptions amount to a transfiguration of matter by spirit (transformation from "corporeality" to a state which is organic and spiritual), and thus to propound an outline of "natural eschatology."[4] This envisages a "natural transfiguration," death, to a great extent, by its purifying function, bringing about the domination of the spirit. At the same time, the Platonist doctrine of fulfillment is countered not merely polemically, but positively, in that the process of spiritualization proceeds radically from matter. In this way, Hengstenberg, perhaps for the first time, applies the law of *gratia supponit naturam* to the resurrection, without, however, laying himself open to the suspicion of confusing theology with gnosis and nature-mysticism.[5] Alois Dempf skilfully takes over the anthropology and cosmology of German idealism (Schelling, Schlegel, Görres) into a Catholic meta-

[1] K. Rahner, *Geist in Welt* (1939). Hans André, *Vom Sinnreich des Lebens.* An ontology of the basic structure of faith, Salzburg; and *Die Kirche als Keimzelle der Weltvergöttlichung.* An outline-structure in the light of biological considerations. The works (Leipzig 1920) of Hedwig Conrad-Martius, and, in the field of history, of Friedrich Heer, for whom all the demons in Christian and Church history originate in an abstract spiritism, that is, one derived from the body, from the "underground," from the *Mater-materia.*

[2] Paul Claudel, "L'Ars poétique, Sur la Présence de Dieu, La Sensation du Divin," *Présence et Prophetie* 1942.

[3] Most recently *Der Lieb und die Letzten Dinge,* Regensburg 1955. A recasting of *Tod und Vollendung,* Regensburg 1938.

[4] *Ibid.,* 18.

[5] "Supernatural transfiguration must, in some way, include the perfections of natural transfiguration, without the specific nature of supernatural transfiguration being put on a level with that of the natural": *Der Leib und die Letzten Dinge,* Regensburg 1955, 156.

physic. Frank-Duquesne (*Cosmos et Gloire,* with prefaces by Claudel and Dom Capelle, Paris 1947) skirts on eastern sophiology, which runs the risk of incorporating indiscriminately natural and supernatural eschatology in a comprehensive religious metaphysic. It is an open question whether Teilhard de Chardin, in his eschatological outlook, succeeds in avoiding a simple incorporation of the eschatological data of revelation into a system of universal cosmic evolution.

In constructing a sound and comprehensive eschatology of man, history and the cosmos, it is the task of Catholic thought to take up the themes of present-day existentialist philosophy and theology. We still lack a complete theology of death,[1] and also a Catholic philosophy and theology of history[2] and the cosmos which is more than a mere outline.

Finally, we may mention the problem of the relationship between Jewish and Christian eschatology, which is as yet secret, but still urgent. Judaism, in reflecting on its own nature, has defined itself as an essentially religious and social messianism of this world (Buber, Baeck, Rosenweig, Achad Haam), with its characteristic "prophetical" linking of social reform (to the point of religious communism) with a "utopian" sense of belonging to God and the covenant alone. The strongest force behind capitalism and communism as well, behind the radical east and the radical west,

---

[1] An important contribution to one is Berlinger's *Das Nichts und der Tod,* Frankfurt. See also Reisenfeld, *La descente dans la mort,* Paris 1950.

[2] Besides the works already cited of Pieper and Daniélou, we should notice Th. Haecker, *Der Christ und die Geschichte,* 1935; Konrad Weiss, *Zum geschichlichen Gethsemani,* 1919; Peter Wust, *Dialektik des Geistes,* 1928; J. Bernhart, *Der Sinn der Geschichte,* 1931.

174

is the Jewish force which, corresponding to its special function and nature, is strongly poised between cultural immanentism (in the bond of "blood and soil") and Christian transcendence: a world shattered, open to what is above the world (Christian), yet guarding against it with every possible means.

But Christ as man is the fulfillment also of Judaism and of its function. Jewish and Christian eschatology belong ultimately together, and it is all the more tragic that, in actual history, they seem to be so opposed. The transition from the Old to the New Testament cannot be taken to mean indifference to the tremendous witness of Israel in the fields of politics and society. The kingdom of God comes because Christ is a man, and a Jew—from above and from without. It is essentially a fruit of the earth, of Mary certainly, but in her of the entire holy people, which, as a real people, has its real function in the world.[1]

[1] For the literature since 1957, see the third edition of *Fragen der Theologie heute,* 1960, 566ff.